The
Seven Years
War

The British at War

at War

General Editor:
Ludovic Kennedy

Rupert Furneaux

The
Seven Years
War

Book Club Associates London

This edition published 1973 by
Book Club Associates
By arrangement with Granada Publishing Ltd.

Copyright © 1973 by Rupert Furneaux

ISBN 246 10514 3

Filmset by Keyspools Limited, Golborne, Lancs
Printed in Great Britain by C. Tinling & Co Ltd,
Prescot & London

Contents

Acknowledgements

The photographs and illustrations in this book are reproduced by kind permission of the following. Those on pages 36 and 179 by the gracious permission of H.M. the Queen; pages 10, 62, 70, 77, 94–5, 121, 122, 146–7, 175, 176, 190, National Army Muséum; pages 26, 28, 33, 34, 51, 88, 101, 112, 168, 181, 186, National Portrait Gallery; pages 12–13, 40, 47, 60–61, 103, 104, 108–9, 115, 118, 123, 126, 134, 139, 140, 182–3, 194–5, 196, National Maritime Museum; pages 18, 21, 37, 67, 84, 111, 158, 165, 202–3, Department of Prints and Drawings, British Museum; pages 52, 56, 57, 59, 64–5, India Office Library and Records; pages 38–9, 44, 53, 80–81, 83, 125, 142, 156, 162, 166, 169, 186–7, 204, Radio Times Hulton Picture Library; pages 31, 54, 63, 148–9, 185, Mansell Collection; pages 93, 96, 129, 137, National Trust, Quebec House; page 30, Wallace Collection; page 14, U.S. Information Service; page 184, Victoria and Albert Museum; page 132, Ashmolean Museum, Oxford; the pictures on page 60 are from *Murshiolerbad* by T. H. Tull Walsh and *Echoes of Old Calcutta* by H. E. Bustead; on page 86, from *Louisbourg 1713–1768* by J. S. McLennon; and on page 193 from the *Gentleman's Magazine* of 1762. Illustration Research Service supplied the pictures. The maps were drawn by Brian and Constance Dear.

Introduction

The Seven Years War marks a turning-point in British history. Not only was it in effect the first world war, but by the end of it Britain had acquired a huge, colonial empire. This empire was to turn Britain's eyes away from Europe, create a power vacuum there which emergent Prussian militarism was soon to fill. So one can say that the echoes of the bells that rang for victory in 1759 have only recently died away.

In this war, as in others, the British lost every battle (or almost every battle) except the last. At the beginning the incompetent Braddock ran into an ambush near Fort Duquesne (today's Pittsburgh), Admiral Byng failed to relieve Minorca (and was shot, Voltaire acidly remarked, 'in order to encourage the others'), the wretched employees of the East India Company stifled in the Black Hole of Calcutta.

In the end, as Rupert Furneaux shows, victory was achieved mainly because of two things; the genius of William Pitt as strategist and politician, and the exercise of British sea-power 'the deadliest weapon' Liddell Hart called it, 'which any nation has wielded through history.'

Ludovic Kennedy

Chapter 1

Fusillade at Great Meadows

The French named it *'La Guerre de Sept Ans'*, though it lasted for nine years. To the Austrians it was the war for Silesia, the piece of territory seized by the greedy Prussian, Frederick. Frederick referred to it as the 'Petticoat War', in derogatory honour of his chief opponents, Maria Theresa, Empress of Austria, Elizabeth, Czarina of Russia, and 'General' Pompadour, the French King's interfering mistress. To the wretched Saxons over whose lands the armies marched, it was the *'Krieg'*, just another war. The Spaniards recognised its true nature by calling it the 'English War', in petulant defiance of the sea robbers who despoiled their colonies. The Americans thought of it as the 'French and Indian War'.

The British described it, at first in derision and later in jubilation when the bells tolled for victory, as 'Pitt's War', in honour of the great minister who planned the campaigns which won an empire. Today it is better known as The Seven Years War. The opening shots were fired on the American frontier, at the order of the man who became its chief beneficiary . . .

The young Major heard the bullets whistle, and thought 'there was something charming in the sound'. Twenty-two-year-old George Washington led a mixed force of Virginia militia and Mingo Indians, one hundred and fifty strong, his mission to oust the French Canadians from the fort they had built at the forks of the Ohio and Allegheny rivers. The banks of the Ohio were disputed territory. The French Canadians and the Virginians each claimed their ownership. Diplomats meeting in Paris had been arguing the frontier line for three years, each side armed with maps which bore no relation to one another. A small French force, led by Ensign Coulon de Jumoville, advanced to intercept the Virginians. De Jumoville, according to the French version of the incident at Great Meadows on 28 May 1754, ran ahead, waving his commission and inviting a parley. He and nine other Frenchmen were killed. The Mingo Indians scalped the dead and rounded up twenty-one prisoners. One Frenchman escaped to tell the tale of assassination and murder.

Washington, short of supplies, awaiting reinforcements and expecting reprisal, retreated to Fort Necessity, where he entrenched his small force. On 3 July Captain Louis Coulon de Villiers, the dead Ensign's brother, came to drive the assassins from the

Opposite Major-General Edward Braddock is mortally wounded on the banks of the Monongahela river, on the American frontier, as his army is crushed and destroyed by the French-led Indians.

dominions of the King of France. Washington was forced to capitulate. Determined to play down the frontier incident, the Frenchmen allowed the Virginians to retreat to their own country,
unaware of the mighty drama their shots had begun.

The fusillade on the Ohio, when the news reached Europe in
August, caused an uneasy stir. The truce had been broken. Shots
had been fired, blood spilled. The adversaries, France and Britain,
tried to minimise the incident. Each called the nations to witness
that the other was the aggressor, a necessary diplomatic finesse

The falls of
Montmorency with
British ships bombarding
the French camp.

for, under the 'Old System' as it was called, each could call on
allies for help if attacked.

These defensive alliances were designed to deter the nations of
Europe from engaging in full-scale war from which no one would
benefit. Peace, it was hoped, could be preserved by the threat of
war, by mutual pledges of assistance. This system failed to prevent
the outbreak of hostilities in 1754 because Britain and France, as
well as being old continental enemies, were also colonial rivals.

The British had established thirteen colonies strung out along   13

George Washington, whose shots fired at Great Meadows on the American frontier precipitated the war which extended to all four known continents and three oceans.

the Atlantic seaboard. The French possessed Canada to their north and Louisiana to their south. They hoped to confine the Americans to the line of the Allegheny Mountains, to prevent their expansion westwards. To achieve that end, they planned to establish a chain of forts in the Ohio valley, linking the Great Lakes and the Mississippi. Their attempt to build Fort Duquesne on the forks of the Ohio had brought George Washington hurrying from Virginia to protect the lands claimed by the 'Ohio Company', as the Virginian venture was called.

The Americans, as it is easiest to call the British Colonists, feared the French threat to their existence. There could be no repose, Benjamin Franklin believed, 'as long as the French are masters of Canada'. The British government embarked upon war deliberately to protect the Americans.

The part played by the Thirteen Colonies in the struggle which finally freed them from the threat of French aggression, and from which they benefited enormously, has been argued by historians. Those who wrote shortly after the great American victory in the War of Independence created the myth that American contributions to the earlier defeat of France had been decisive. Modern American historians are more realistic. They recognise that without British regular soldiers, artillery and sea-power the Colonists were doomed to French envelopment. They were ill-equipped and ill-trained to fight a war against professionals.

Fortunately for the Americans, the British ministers understood the nature of the inevitable struggle with France and Spain for the trade and commerce of the New World. Its possession would bring wealth and power, its loss poverty and slavery.

The French feared that ownership of North America and the sugar islands of the Caribbean would give Britain power to over-shadow her European rivals. They hoped to achieve all they wanted by peaceful means. This French policy played into the hands of the British ministers who wished to confine the struggle to limited operations on the American frontier, without repercussions in Europe.

The French seemed to be the strongest power in North America, despite the disparity in population. Fewer than fifty-five thousand Frenchmen opposed more than a million Americans. Though small in number the Canadians were more united than the mutually jealous and disunited American colonists.

The French Canadians held the strategic advantage by their possession of the inland waterways, the chief rivers and lakes, the only feasible means of transport through the trackless wilderness. But they were confined to a single outlet to the Atlantic, the St Lawrence seaway, guarded by the powerful bastion, the fortress of Louisbourg on Cape Breton island. They relied on the Atlantic Ocean for their supplies and reinforcements. Thus the security of Canada and its survival as a French colony depended upon sea-power, the decisive weapon which France lacked. 15

France, with a population of twenty million, was the greatest military power in Europe. Britain with less than eight million people could mobilise only a small army. Secure in her sea-girt isolation, she did not require a large land-force so long as she commanded the seas.

Another factor operated in Britain's favour. France was beset by insolvency and social unrest. Britain was strong financially, her trade booming, her people exuberant, confident of their destiny.

Had the conduct of the war remained under the control of the Whig oligarchy who ruled England, the struggle with France might have ended indecisively, with each side bartering the spoils at the conclusion of peace. Fortunately, as it turned out, the war opened with a series of disasters. They brought to power the one man who was capable of understanding its true nature and how it should be waged. But in the autumn of 1754 it seemed unlikely that he would have any say, far less rule, in the matter.

For months William Pitt 'the Elder', or the Earl of Chatham as he subsequently became, had been morose, melancholy, indolent, ill and despairing of his own future and that of his country. Following twenty years of effort, his political career seemed over. He had challenged the Establishment, forced it to recognise his talents and had been quietly dropped. Lesser men were passing him by. Aged forty-six, bitter and resentful, Pitt determined to forsake politics. In September 1754, following Washington's ignominious failure on the Ohio, Pitt left London on a round of country house visits.

On a sudden whim he ordered his coachman to drive him to Wotton in Buckinghamshire, the home of his friend George Grenville. They had known each other since their schooldays at Eton, and Pitt had been visiting Wotton for twenty years. He had known George's sister, Hester, since she was fourteen. She was now thirty-three and still unmarried, as was Pitt. Good-looking, poised, the essence of a great lady, Hester could have made several excellent matches. Admired and courted, she rejected all advances, possibly because she loved the man who seemed blind to her admiration. Preoccupied with public affairs and unsure of his financial position, Pitt may have feared to unlock the flood-gates of emotion.

One late September morning, William and Hester sauntered down to the lake. They returned to the house engaged, and were married on 24 November. Pitt's idyllic and happy marriage changed history. He returned to Parliament invigorated and galvanised. For six years he was at the height of his powers.

Following a spell in the army, as a dashing but peace-time Cornet of Horse, Pitt had entered Parliament in 1735, the indispensable source of advancement. Lacking a 'connection', the control of a collection of boroughs, he quickly made a name for himself both as an orator and as the vitriolic critic of the all-powerful Whig Junta and of the King, the ageing George II.

To achieve his ambition and lead his country to victory in the struggle for world dominion which he foresaw, Pitt needed to interpret and express the true spirit and vigour of England, the inarticulate hopes of the patriots who foresaw England's manifest destiny. The new international giant was stirring. England was becoming the first industrialised nation, manufacturing goods to sell in her fast-expanding colonial markets in exchange for the raw materials supplied by her monopoly of trade with the Thirteen American Plantations, Nova Scotia, Newfoundland, Hudson Bay, Bermuda and the Bahamas, the Caribbean islands of Barbados and Jamaica, the Leeward Islands and Honduras. India and Africa were served by private trading companies, and England owned two strategic bases, Gibraltar and Minorca in the Mediterranean. The trade from which England gained her wealth and which created the sinews with which to wage aggressive war depended upon sea-power.

For seven years, from 1735 to 1742, Pitt mercilessly attacked the government, accusing it of surrendering to 'foreign arrogance' and criticising England's naval and military incapabilities. The ministers quailed before his terrible voice, the King cursed his arrogance, but since he lacked a connection Pitt's invective proved unavailing. New ministers, hoping to tame the violent back-bencher, brought him into the government first as Secretary of War, a routine post, and later as Paymaster of the Forces, a potentially lucrative office which Pitt held through twelve years of scrupulous honesty. No sooner had he achieved this small measure of recognition than he was struck down by illness, described as severe gout but in reality the first signs of that manic-depressive insanity which plagued his latter years. On his recovery he became the nominal henchman of the new Chief Minister, the Duke of Newcastle, who despite his avowed determination to have no minister in his government 'who tells me he is wiser than I am', apparently feared Pitt less in office than in opposition. Upon a Cabinet reshuffle Pitt was dismissed, losing £4,000 a year but gaining his freedom to criticise the government as Britain's disasters mounted.

The Duke of Newcastle understood the situation on the American frontier and was determined to support the colonists. He believed that the French government would repudiate the Canadians' provocative action in building forts on the Ohio in the disputed neutral territory. Should hostilities continue, he hoped to limit warfare to the American frontier.

The Duke had voiced the 'Imperial' idea at a Cabinet meeting held on 29 June 1754, six weeks before news was received in London of Washington's humiliation on the Ohio.

The first point we have laid down is, that the Colonists must not be abandoned, that our rights and possessions in North America must be maintained and the French obliged to desist from their hostile attempt to dispossess us.

The Duke of Newcastle, Thomas Pelham Holles, has been portrayed as a ridiculous figure, the corrupt party-manager, the timid politician, who sought to retain personal power in the face of every humiliation. He has suffered in contrast to the heroic Pitt. Irresolute and bewildered as he may have been, Newcastle understood the strategic principle and the necessity for action.

He invited the Duke of Cumberland, the Captain-General of the army, and the King's son, the victor of the battle of Culloden over the Young Pretender in 1746, to formulate a plan for the protection of the North American colonies. Cumberland recommended to George II the recruitment of Colonial forces and the despatch of two weak English regiments, about eight hundred soldiers, under the command of Major-General Edward Braddock.

Major-General Edward Braddock, the 'unfortunate chief who perhaps merited the least of the blame', as George Washington described him.

Braddock reached Virginia in February 1755, unaware that a copy of his orders had been secured by bribery, transmitted to Paris and sent to Canada, and totally ignorant of the special problems of colonial warfare. An elderly guardsman, a rigid disciplinarian, a stereotyped, unimaginative though courageous soldier, Braddock was expected to supervise four independent expeditions; his own to batter into submission Fort Duquesne at the forks of the Ohio; that led by the energetic Governor of Massachusetts, William Shirley, to capture Fort Niagara at the junction of Lakes Erie and Ontario; another under the expert in Indian warfare, William Johnson, to take Crown Point on Lake Champlain; and the fourth, led by Robert Monckton, to seize Fort Beauséjour at the head of the Bay of Fundy.

Braddock and his subordinate commanders would drive the French Canadians from the lands where they had encroached. The four forts would provide advance posts against future French aggression. By these simultaneous thrusts, the tables would be turned and the French would be hemmed in, being denied their advance bases. The Colonial line of defence would be extended from the headwaters of the Ohio to the Gulf of St Lawrence.

It was a good plan, typically English in its conception and design, entirely beyond the capabilities of that nation at the start of a war. To achieve success it required considerable preparation, organisation and military efficiency. To capture these forts necessitated campaigning over a huge area, by marches through trackless forests, by narrow trails, laborious portages and the navigation of exposed and often turbulent waterways. The forts, having been captured, would have to be supplied and reinforced, and would be isolated during the harsh winter months.

The plan required full Colonial co-operation.

The prodigious efforts and remarkable military skill shown by the rebel colonists in the later War of Independence has obscured the unpalatable fact that the Americans, in the earlier struggle against the common foe, made only a small contribution to victory. The Congress called at Albany, New York, had failed to persuade the thirteen separate colonies to unite, or even to co-operate by raising their militia and marching them to each other's aid. The Assemblies were loath to vote money to raise and equip soldiers who when they were mobilised proved inefficient, discontented and mutinous. Virginia for example, one of the richest colonies, highly vulnerable to Indian raids and with a paper strength of twenty-seven thousand militiamen, could mobilise only six hundred men.

The fine promises made by the Colonial Governors had led the home government to expect whole-hearted Colonial co-operation. Braddock soon learned how illusory these promises were. He complained of the 'supineness and unreasonable economy' of the colonies, of the 'general falsehood and dishonesty that prevails among them', and of the 'inexcusable behaviour' of their governments. He told his government that he was 'in despair' of complying with its orders, 'from the jealousy of the people and the disunion of the several colonies as well among themselves as one with another'.

Why were the Americans so short-sighted when their security was at stake? Only a few years before, in 1745, an American expedition had captured the French fortress of Louisbourg, an amazing feat. At the end of that war the British had swapped the vital fortress for Madras in India, which in American eyes was a paltry gain. The Americans feared a repetition of such bargaining. 19

Added to that the Americans were forced in the new French and Indian war to rely on British help. Fiercely independent, they resented British superiority.

General Braddock obstinately refused to take advice from these Americans who were experienced in frontier warfare. He believed he could defeat the French and their Indian allies by the tactics employed in Europe. For centuries battles had been fought there in a traditional manner, on flat open plains intersected by convenient roads. He had no conception of the dangers of the ambush, the classic Indian strategy. He might have defeated the numerically inferior Frenchmen had he commanded high quality troops. Alas, with typical parsimony, and belittlement of their enemy, the British government had supplied him with two of the worst regiments in the army. They were made up largely of drafts from other regiments, of men of whom their colonels wished to be rid.

Braddock's troops resented serving in America and disliked everything they found there, the lack of grog-ships, the scarcity of accessible women, the greed of the men, the heat, the rough territory and above all the Indians. The colonial volunteers brought Braddock's force up to thirty-two hundred men. 'But scarcely any military service could be expected' of these colonials, he complained. Few of the American farmers, merchants, labourers and fishermen had had any frontier experience, fewer still any experience of command. Washington was one of the few exceptions and he had yet to prove his military genius. He joined Braddock as a volunteer aide. Braddock rejected his advice to tread warily, insisting that regular platoon firing and military discipline would be an adequate defence against skulking Indians and ill-led Frenchmen.

Braddock despaired of getting started. The two hundred and fifty waggons and the two thousand five hundred saddle-horses he required were not forthcoming. Each heavy gun required seven horses to drag it. Without these cannon Fort Duquesne could not be battered into submission. Its defences were known from the map drawn by the Virginian Captain Robert Stobo, one of the hostages left the year before by George Washington. Stobo managed to smuggle it out and send it to Braddock. The French found it in his baggage and traced it to Stobo whom they accused of espionage.

More helpful to Braddock would have been a map of the three-hundred-mile route he had been persuaded to follow by Governor Dinwiddie of Virginia, in preference to the more direct road from Pennsylvania. The backwoods country had not been surveyed

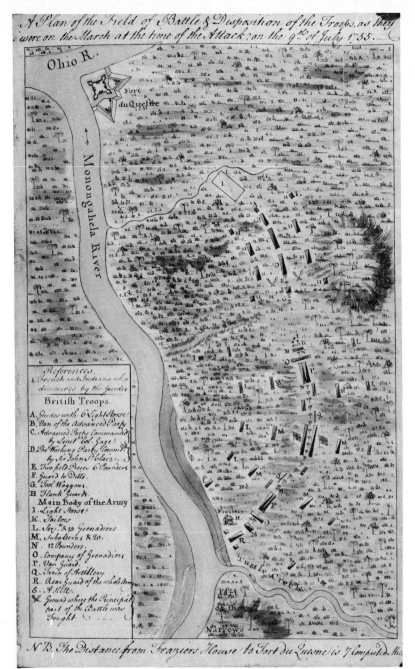

A Plan of the Field of Battle & Disposition of the Troops, as they were on the March at the time of the Attack, on the 9th of July 1755.

Ohio R.

Fort du Quesne

Monongahela River

References.
1. French and Indians when discovered by the guides

British Troops.

A. Guides with 6 Light Horse
B. Van of the Advanced Party
C. Advanced Party Commanded by Lieut Col. Gage
D. The Working Party Commanded by Sir John St Clair
E. Two field Pieces 6 Pounders
F. Guard to Ditto
G. Tool Waggons
H. Flank Guards

Main Body of the Army

I. Light Horse
K. Sailors
L. Serj.ts & 10 Grenadiers
M. Subalterns & 20.
N. 12 Pounders
O. Company of Grenadiers
P. Van Guard
Q. Train of Artillery
R. Rear Guard of the whole Army
S. A Hill
Y. Ground where the Principal part of the Battle was fought

Fraziers

Turtle Creek

Fort

Narrows

N.B. The Distance from Fraziers House to Fort du Quesne is 7 Computed Miles

The Monongahela river and Wills Creek. The map drawn by Robert Orme to show the scene of the disaster with which the war opened.

21

and was sparsely populated. Between Braddock and his objective lay numerous creeks and rivers, swamps, trackless forests, and fifty miles of mountains, some twenty-five hundred feet high.

Waggons and teams were finally procured through the resource of Benjamin Franklin. The famous sage held the office of Deputy Postmaster of the North American Colonies and was the most influential man in Pennsylvania. He persuaded the German farmers to hire out waggons with four horses each at fifteen shillings a day, an exorbitant sum which produced a hundred and fifty waggons and fifteen hundred horses. These waggons were driven by colonial teamsters who found themselves subject to military discipline. One waggoner, Daniel Morgan, fell foul of a British officer and was goaded into striking him, a terrible crime. Morgan was given five hundred lashes of the cat-o'-nine-tails, a punishment he miraculously survived. Morgan had his revenge twenty-five years later. He raised and commanded his own corps of riflemen, all crack shots, in the Revolutionary War, and was largely responsible for the decisive American victory at Saratoga.

Braddock's column got under way on 26 April, making eighteen miles a day. The waggons were insufficient to carry all the supplies and had to be shuttled back and forth from each magazine. Three hundred American axe-men marched ahead of the convoy, blazing a trail through the wilderness and making a passable road twelve feet wide, 'an eighth wonder of the world' as one historian has called it. Progress slowed as the soldiers splashed through swamps, built bridges, stumbled over hills and cut through forests. Stragglers and foragers were ambushed and scalped by marauding Indians. Braddock had few Indian scouts. The so-called 'friendly' Indians had stayed clear of the expedition, determined to remain neutral until one side or the other had won a decisive victory. The loyal scouts reported that Fort Duquesne was held by a garrison of fifty men, and that another nine hundred were expected.

The column reached Fort Necessity on 13 June. Braddock sought Washington's advice and was urged to push ahead with a small force. This was exactly the course of action which a year before had brought disaster.

Leading fifteen hundred men and leaving the rest of his army forty miles behind, Braddock reached the banks of the Monongahela river, seven to eight miles from Fort Duquesne, on 9 July, expecting to find the French and their Indian allies waiting in ambush. Captain Jean Dumas had decided to sally out to attack the invaders rather than wait behind his defences which were inadequate to withstand artillery assault. He commanded three hundred French regular soldiers and about eight hundred Indians. When they clamoured that there was no hope, he told them 'the English are going to throw themselves into the lion's mouth'.

Braddock crossed the river unopposed, falsely confident that the French were unaware of his approach whereas his column had been spied on for many days by the French Indians. By 8.00 a.m. the column with its waggons and guns was safely across the river. There was no sign of the enemy. The wooded hill ahead was silent and empty. Dumas' Indians skulked in the trees watching the British. As they toiled up the slope, Dumas ordered his men to spread out in order to encircle the British flanks. Spotting shadowy figures moving through the trees, the soldiers opened fire. From behind every rock and tree the Indians poured devastating fire upon the conspicuous red-coated soldiers on the open slopes. The slaughter was prodigious. The ill-disciplined soldiers broke and fled.

A quarter of a mile behind, Braddock heard the firing; the popping of muskets grew heavier, the volleys died away. He ordered up eight hundred more men and three 12-pounders. Marching forward they met the fleeing advance guard, mingling in a tangle of guns, waggons, teamsters and soldiers. Those behind pushed forward, those in front pushed backwards. The struggling mass grew bigger as more men came running. The Indians poured their fire into the mêlée.

Braddock galloped up. The road was jammed, the soldiers twelve and fourteen deep. 'March on,' he ordered, 'Fire.' 'Fire where?' asked the bewildered men. Braddock rode back and forth wielding the flat of his sword, ordering his soldiers to form line, face the enemy, fire volleys. Men were toppling right and left, the ground was littered with the dead and dying, the wounded were writhing in agony. No Indians could be seen, yet they picked off the mounted officers resplendent in their gorgeous uniforms. The Colonel of the 44th Regiment, Sir Peter Hackell, and his ensign son were both killed. Washington came to Braddock. 'Scatter three hundred marksmen in the trees, fight the Indians on their own terms', he urged. A few soldiers ran towards the trees.

It was now four o'clock and the afternoon was sticky with heat. Half the British force had been killed or wounded. The ground was thick with dead. Braddock ordered retreat. Four horses had been killed under him, and he was in the act of mounting a fifth when he was struck in the side. The bullet penetrated his lungs. Washington helped him to a cart. Braddock asked for his pistols, and to be left   23 on the field. He did not wish to live. Ignoring their dying General's protests the orderlies led the cart away, guiding it across the river, where the ford was choked with soldiers, waggons and guns. Behind came the yelling, exultant Indians, tomahawking the living, scalping the dead. They did not pursue beyond the river. They returned to the fort whooping and shouting, waving their scalps and bringing their prisoners who that night were tied to stakes with fires kindled at their feet. The tormentors poked them with blazing torches and red-hot irons. Captain Stobo, safe in his cell, listened to their blood-curdling shrieks.

The panic-stricken British soldiers struggled through the night, throwing away their muskets and heavy coats, abandoning waggons and artillery. Braddock was dazed. 'Who would have thought it?' he asked. He died next day and was buried in the road, twenty miles from the scene of the action. Washington ordered the waggons to drive over the road in order to obliterate the grave for fear that the Indians would find it. Braddock's scalp would be a trophy indeed.

The battle had lasted for less than three hours. The British had lost two-thirds of their force; a thousand men had been killed and wounded, including sixty-three officers. Washington blamed the defeat on 'the dastardly behaviour of the English soldiers'. He called Braddock 'the unfortunate chief who perhaps merited the least of the blame', an estimate which historians have chosen to ignore. Another colonial officer was less charitable. He attributed the disaster to 'the pride and ignorance of that general who came from England'. Braddock looked upon the Americans as dogs, and would never hear anything that was said to him. 'We often tried to tell him of the danger he was in, but he never appeared pleased with us, and that was the reason that a great many of our warriors left him and would not serve under his command.' Benjamin Franklin called Braddock a brave man who had too much confidence in his regular troops and too mean an opinion of both Americans and Indians. When he learned of the disaster on the Monongahela, the English diarist and wit Horace Walpole, safe and snug in his suburban sanctuary, described it as the longest battle ever fought against nobody.

The overall command in North America devolved upon William Shirley. Though a lawyer and not a soldier, he showed considerable generalship. Of the four expedition leaders Robert Monckton, the British Colonel of the Royal American Regiment, had the easiest task. He was able to transport his two thousand Rangers by water to the Bay of Fundy for the assault on Fort

Beauséjour, which guarded the narrow isthmus of Chignecto joining Nova Scotia to the mainland and was thus of considerable strategic importance. Due in part to Thomas Picknon, the fort's commissariat officer who betrayed its secrets, the garrison surrendered without a blow. It was the first break in the chain of the two-thousand-mile French defence system which stretched from the Gulf of St Lawrence to the Gulf of Mexico. The fort's capture led to the expulsion from Nova Scotia of the French peasants, the Acadians as they were called. They had steadfastly refused to take the Oath of Allegiance to the British Crown, and now they were deported and scattered throughout the Thirteen Colonies.

Though it failed to achieve its objective, the capture of Crown Point on Lake Champlain, William Johnson's expedition was not entirely a failure. He achieved the appearance of success. Half Irish and half Indian by birth, Johnson made up for his lack of military experience by his standing with the local Indians, and his knowledge of the region in which he was ordered to campaign. He brought his force of three thousand raw militiamen to Fort William Henry on the southern shore of Lake George, but no preparations had been made to build boats by which to convey the soldiers up that lake, across the portage at Fort Ticonderoga and up Lake Champlain. While Johnson delayed, the French acted. They knew of Johnson's plans from Braddock's captured papers. Baron Dieskau, leaving two thousand militia to guard Crown Point, sailed southwards with fifteen hundred regulars, landing close to Fort William Henry. Although he learned that Johnson commanded a superior force, he was loath to retreat without striking a blow. He marched into an ambush, lost half his men and was himself wounded and taken prisoner. Johnson failed to profit from his victory. On the approach of winter most of his troops deserted and he was forced to withdraw, leaving a small garrison to hold the fort. His limited achievement was recognised by the British government, avid for some small success, by the grant of a baronetcy and the gift of £5,000.

Shirley had reached Albany in central New York when he heard of Braddock's disaster. It made a difficult task (the capture of Fort Niagara) even harder for it released French troops to protect the vital fort. Success depended upon speed, and of that Shirley's soldiers were incapable. His twenty-four hundred men were composed of raw levies, dispirited by the news of Braddock's defeat. There were insufficient boats to transport them down the Mohawk river and across the lake to Oswego, a distance of two hundred and fifty miles. The boatmen proved mutinous, many 25

Vice-Admiral Sir Edward Boscawen who did either too much or too little when he attacked the French fleet off the Newfoundland Banks before war had been officially declared.

deserted, and the expected Indian help was not forthcoming, for Johnson had recruited the tribesmen. Shirley brought his army to Oswego; Fort Niagara lay one hundred and fifty miles across Lake Ontario. He was forced to delay to build sloops in order to counter those possessed by the French. It was already 2 September, and the campaigning season was nearing its end; the lake was lashed by torrential rains and tempestuous winds.

Shirley decided to postpone his attack on Fort Niagara for another year, a wise decision for which he was severely criticised and eventually deposed from his command. The French had ample warning of his progress and presence at Oswego. They assembled fourteen hundred regulars and twelve hundred militia at Forts Niagara and Frontenac. Had Shirley advanced he would have been caught between two foes. Leaving seven hundred men to repair and hold Oswego, he returned to Albany, from where he reported to the British government, urging a war of conquest rather than defence.

Britain and France were still nominally at peace. Both nations were prepared to employ force to protect their interests in North America. The French government, it was learned in London, planned to send seventy-eight companies of their best-trained soldiers to Canada. These three thousand disciplined troops would turn the balance in France's favour. Should these reinforcements be allowed to cross the Atlantic? At a Cabinet meeting held on 24 March 1755, the momentous decision was taken to waylay the French transports off Cape Breton. Vice-Admiral Edward Boscawen sailed from Portsmouth on 27 April, commanding eleven ships of the line. The French transports, escorted by fourteen battleships, sailed from Brest six days later. They were spotted and reported by British frigates.

The Comte de la Motte's fleet reached the Grand Banks off Newfoundland on 25 May. His ships were scattered by gales and became lost in fog. The weather saved the fleet from total disaster. Boscawen sighted three French ships on 6 June. 'Are we at peace or war?' hailed the Frenchmen. 'At peace, at peace,' shouted Captain Howe of the *Dunkirk*. He fired broadsides into the *Lys* and the *Dauphin Royal*. Both vessels surrendered. 'Behold! a very singular kind of peace, or rather a war declared in a very singular manner', remarked Captain Lorgeril of the *Lys*. The British captured three ships carrying ten companies of soldiers. The surviving transports, one carrying the governor of New France, the Marquis de Vaudreuil, and another the army commander, the Marquis de Montcalm, escaped in the fog and reached Quebec. De la Motte eluded the British fleet and returned to Brest.

'We have done either too little or too much,' remarked Lord Hardwicke, the Lord Chancellor, when the Cabinet met to consider the implications of Boscawen's hollow victory. The ministers decided that it was more than ever necessary to challenge the French in European waters. Admiral Hawke was ordered to attack French ships wherever he found them. The French had won the first round, but they were dangerously weak at sea; their life-line to Canada was in peril.

Chapter 2

"To Encourage the Others"

Britain's abortive attempt to stage a 'Pearl Harbor' by striking a secret blow to prevent French reinforcements from reaching Canada did not lead to a declaration of war, despite the provocation. Louis XV merely withdrew his ambassador from London. Both nations needed to bolster their positions in Europe. By the 'Old System' France and Prussia had been allied against Britain and Austria. Britain's European policy was conditioned by two factors, the neutrality of the Netherlands, part of the Austrian Empire, and her Achilles heel, the King's Hanoverian Electorate. It was vulnerable to French attack and could be held as a pawn to be exchanged for some British conquest. As his family heritage Hanover had great sentimental value for George II. He would not agree to Britain entering any war unless the safety of his Electorate was guaranteed.

The 'Reversal of Alliances' brought about in 1756 stemmed from the Austrians' desire to acquire the military strength of France, a more tangible asset than the naval might of Britain. The ground had been prepared by Chancellor Kaunitz when he was Austrian Ambassador in Paris. To clinch the alliance, Empress Maria Theresa appealed to Madame de Pompadour, the French King's influential mistress. This feminine intrigue, into which the Czarina Elizabeth was drawn, isolated Prussia, forcing Frederick to seek an alliance with Britain. George II welcomed him as a partner as a means for securing the safety of Hanover, overcoming his dislike of his nephew whom he had called that 'proud, overbearing prince'.

The combination of France and Austria, the two great European military powers, appeared to provide overwhelming land-power. This was an illusion created by the size of their armies. Their officers were recruited exclusively from the ranks of the nobility, and promotion was subject to the whims of their female 'generals'— Maria Theresa who refused to dismiss old and loyal servants, and Madame de Pompadour who preferred nonentities rather than officers of experience. As a result Frederick was faced by timid, mediocre officers, which partly accounts for the amazing results he achieved.

Frederick Hohenzollern possessed a genius for war and for making enemies. His malicious jests at Maria Theresa's piety, her husband's loose morals, Czarina Elizabeth's taste for vodka and virile aides-de-camp, and Pompadour's humble birth offended these powerful women and made them his implacable enemies. Between them they ruled vast populations, overwhelming in

Opposite King George II (1683–1760) in whose reign the war opened, and who came, after early suspicion, to support his great war minister, William Pitt.

29

numbers compared with Prussia's meagre four and a half million people. Throughout the war her soldiers were outnumbered by three to one. Numbers were an important factor in eighteenth century warfare, in which thousands died from disease or from their wounds. In this process of attrition Frederick was bound to lose. But he proved himself the greatest general of the age. In his previous war with Austria he had perfected his army, trained his soldiers, modernised his artillery, and, an unheard-of innovation in those aristocratic days, promoted his officers by merit. Frederick was his own general and head of state, able to subordinate policy to strategy, an inestimable advantage, especially in a war against allies who lacked common frontiers. Thus while it seemed that Frederick must be overwhelmed by the numbers of his foes, he managed somehow to extricate himself from the mess into which his aggressive tactics so often brought him. Time and again the allied generals helped him out.

Above Maria Theresa, Empress of Austria, who fought to regain the province of Silesia taken by Frederick the Great.

By allying herself with Austria, her traditional enemy, France had made a bad bargain. She had allowed herself to be drawn into a central European struggle in which she had no concern, for no particular reason other than the acquisition of ports in the Netherlands, a possible threat to Britain. In Frederick Britain had gained a powerful partner who could keep France occupied in Europe while she seized the French overseas colonies. Though strong on land, mustering an army of two hundred thousand trained soldiers, France was dangerously weak at sea, possessing only sixty ships of the line and thirty-one frigates to oppose one hundred ships and sixty frigates from Britain. Her maritime situation was rendered more desperate by her lack of trained seamen and her traditional policy whereby no officer lacking noble birth could rise to high command. Only if Spain joined in the struggle could the Bourbon kings attain numerical superiority, and the Spanish King proved cool to French pleas for help against the parvenu aggressor who threatened both their colonial empires.

Opposite Madame de Pompadour, the French King's interfering mistress, the 'General of the Armies', who by her intrigues contributed to the defeat of France.

Britain and Prussia confirmed their alliance in January 1756 by the Convention of Westminster. France and Austria sealed their partnership by the First Treaty of Versailles. Each contracting party undertook to march to the defence of the other if attacked.

Frederick precipitated the struggle by invading neutral Saxony, while claiming that he was only forestalling Austria's design to seize that land as a vantage point in order to regain her lost Silesian province. Frederick had occupied Silesia in the previous war. When the Saxon King protested that Frederick's conduct was 'without example', the Prussian cynically answered, 'I think not, 31 but even if it were so, are you not aware that I pride myself on being original?' Britain pretended to be outraged by her ally's ruthless act. To the French her protestations of innocence rang hollow. During 1755 the Royal Navy had captured one hundred and ten French merchant ships valued with their cargoes at £6,000,000, thus crippling French trade. Even more serious was the French loss of eight thousand sailors, trained seamen who might have manned the additional ships they were busy constructing, too late to be effective.

The French massed 118 infantry battalions and twenty-eight squadrons of cavalry on the Channel coast, threatening invasion. The British government panicked, hiring twenty thousand Hanoverians and Hessians to bolster its thirty thousand strong army. Pitt dismissed the invasion threat as chimerical, the reliance on German mercenaries an insult to national pride. Possibly realising that lacking sheltered harbours they could stage only a nuisance raid across the Channel, the French switched to strike at Britain's weakest point, the Mediterranean. The British garrison on the island of Minorca, theoretically thirty-three hundred strong, had been reduced by leave-taking to twenty-eight hundred men, commanded by the eighty-four-year-old General William Blakeney.

The efficient British intelligence system, the spies recruited by the Duke of Newcastle, reported in February 1756 that the French Toulon fleet was preparing to transport fifteen thousand soldiers to attack Minorca, one of the Balearic islands. The Duc de Richelieu would command the army, and the Marquis de la Galissonière the fleet of twelve ships of the line, all recently commissioned and in fighting trim. He was France's most experienced admiral. As a soldier (in France land and sea commands were interchangeable) he had planned the construction of the Ohio forts to block American westward expansion.

To counter this threat to the Mediterranean base, Admiral John Byng was ordered to Portsmouth to prepare and take to sea ten ships of the line. Byng, aged fifty-two, stood next in flag-rank to Lord Anson, the First Lord of the Admiralty. Byng had considerable sea experience in both the Atlantic and the Mediterranean, and he was a reasonable choice for this important command despite his own rather lukewarm acceptance of the job. To the formal acknowledgement of his orders he added his gratuitous and, as it transpired, dangerous remark that 'I shall think myself fortunate if I am so happy to succeed in this undertaking'. His ill-advised words were later held to show that Byng

William Pitt the Elder,
later the Earl of
Chatham, the architect
of British victory in the
Seven Years War.
After R. Brompton

Robert Clive, the victor
of Plassey. *From the
painting by Nathaniel
Dance*

lacked courage and had no heart for the venture.

Byng's reluctance to accept the appointment was due to the condition of the ships he found awaiting him at Portsmouth. Eight were unfit for sea and four were undermanned. He was expressly ordered not to take men from the other ships in the harbour. They were needed for the cruisers destined to prey upon French merchant ships. This restriction was finally relaxed, and though Byng succeeded in finding seven hundred additional seamen, his ships were still four hundred men short of complement when he sailed on 7 April.

Byng reached Gibraltar after a stormy passage on 2 May, to learn that de la Galissonière had arrived off Minorca on 16 April and Richelieu, having captured Port Mahon, the island's capital, was besieging St Philip's Castle at the harbour mouth. Governor Thomas Fowke had been ordered to supply Byng with troops. While he did not absolutely refuse to send them, Fowke persuaded Byng that they were needed to defend Gibraltar in the unlikely eventuality that the French, having captured Minorca, would proceed there. Byng was at fault in not insisting on their embarkation. He could have landed them on Minorca, where they might have jeopardised the French occupation of the island. Byng added the three ships of the line he found at Gibraltar to his fleet.

Byng, now commanding thirteen ships, sailed the six hundred miles to Minorca, coming in sight of the island on 19 May. The British flag flew above St Philip's Castle. Its garrison was exchanging shots with the French land batteries. Byng sighted the French fleet at 6.00 a.m. next day. Although slightly superior in numbers, Byng's ships were outclassed by the French ships in weight of metal, construction and condition. His manoeuvres were hampered by the Admiralty's Fighting Instructions, an obscure code of naval behaviour, and by the ineffectual British signalling system. Each admiral on assuming command of a fleet adopted his own set of flag signals; their ambiguity and newness often left the captains in doubt of their commander's true intentions.

Byng faced another difficulty. To save Minorca he needed to challenge and defeat the French fleet, a difficult feat because French admirals were expressly ordered to avoid battle in order to achieve 'ulterior objectives'. De la Galissonière needed to protect the army on shore and keep open communications with Toulon. He did not need to risk battle. To achieve the avoidance of action, the French had evolved two techniques. They manoeuvred

35

Frederick II, King of Prussia, who earned the title of the 'Great' by his astounding victories against fearful odds.

their fleet in beautiful formation, like a stately dance, keeping out of range of the dreaded British broadsides while they destroyed the enemies' masts and rigging with their stern chase guns. This evasive action and long range bombardment was designed to cripple the opposing fleet and immobilise it. Thus, to bring de la Galissonière to decisive battle, Byng needed to manoeuvre his ships very skilfully.

According to the accepted and perverse canons of the period, 36 Byng's tactical dispositions were entirely correct. Risking the effects of the superior French fire-power, he offered battle as every British naval officer was expected to do. He signalled his captains to adopt the accepted tactic of diagonal approach, to bring his ships to fall upon the enemy's rear at the point of intersection with its centre. Misreading their Admiral's signals, and hidebound by the shibboleth of the 'unbroken line', the cardinal dogma of the Fighting Instructions, some captains drew ahead to close the extended French line, ship for ship. Divining Byng's true intention, de la Galissonière held back his van to protect his rear. As a result Byng's ships straggled into action one by one leaving his flagship, the *Ramillies*, isolated. This confusion allowed the French to punish the British ships. Four vessels were severely damaged. The engagement, for it was no more, had begun at 2.30 p.m. and was over by five o'clock. Though technically Byng had 'won the day' by forcing his ships between the French fleet and the shore, he had failed to relieve Minorca. His strength had been reduced and he had achieved nothing.

Byng had still some small chance of fulfilling his orders. He could have tried to intercept the French supply line to Toulon, or even blockaded that port. Preferring to believe that Gibraltar was in danger, he returned there. On his arrival he wrote to Lord Anson claiming a tactical victory.

Admiral John Byng, the unfortunate British Admiral who was shot 'to encourage the others' after he had failed to relieve the island of Minorca.

It had become known in Britain that Minorca had been occupied and St Philip's Castle was under siege. News of Byng's relief expedition was anxiously awaited. The arrival of his earlier despatch, dated 4 May, from Gibraltar, did little to allay apprehension. Byng's failure to embark troops led King George to claim, 'This man will not fight'. This royal judgement appeared to be confirmed when on 3 June a copy of de la Galissonière's despatch was received from Paris. The French Admiral stated that the English ships had suffered considerably and had withdrawn from the battle, 'None of their ships having stood the fire of ours for long.' In other words, Byng had lacked aggression. St Philip's Castle fell to the French on 27 June.

The Duke of Newcastle and his ministerial colleagues feared that blame for the loss of Minorca would fall upon them. Byng might claim that he had been given poor ships with which to do a difficult job. To protect themselves the ministers raised a clamour against the cowardly admiral, the man who would not fight. Byng's final despatch, received on 23 June, placed the ministers in a quandary. Taken as a whole it justified his conduct, so they overcame that fearful hazard by printing only half of it and suppressing the vital paragraphs. By a master-stroke they managed to

show that while all the other ships had suffered damage and casualties, Byng's flag-ship had escaped unscathed. Not a man had been killed or wounded. He had kept well out of the battle.

Byng was informed that 'His Majesty is displeased with your conduct', and ordered to return to England. He reached Portsmouth on 26 July, naturally assuming that his despatch had been published in full, and in expectation of an apology. Instead he was arrested, clapped in irons and confined in a room without a bed. He was

A contemporary cartoon satirising British public anxiety about the loss of Minorca.

tried by court martial for having failed to do 'his utmost to relieve St Philip's Castle', a crime for which the Twelfth Article of War decreed death. The court found Byng guilty, recommending him to mercy. King George refused a reprieve. Pitt, who had by now taken office in his first administration, tried to save Byng. Whether he intervened from a sense of justice or in order to blacken the previous government is uncertain. Pitt told the King that the House of Commons was in favour of a reprieve. 'You have taught

The execution of Admiral Byng, an event which King George II refused to stay despite the intercession of William Pitt.

me to look for the sense of my subjects in another place than the House of Commons,' George II retorted. Byng was shot to death on the deck of the *St George*, a ship on which he had once served, on 14 March, 'to encourage the others' as Voltaire cynically remarked. It would have been more apt had he said that Byng had become the scapegoat for the Duke of Newcastle's misgovernment.

On the fall of Minorca, Britain declared war on France, accusing that nation of wanton aggression.

The disasters mounted. In India, where the rival commercial companies strove for mastery, the British East India Company was forced to abandon Calcutta, where the Nawab of Bengal, Surajah Dowlah, thrust 145 Britons into a single dungeon, the 'Black Hole'. Twenty-three survived the stifling June night.

In North America, Shirley was superseded as Commander-in-Chief by the Earl of Loudon who arrived too late in the season either to save Oswego, which fell to the French led now by the energetic Montcalm, or to advance, as he intended, on Fort Ticonderoga at the head of Lake George. With the approach of winter, he was forced to abandon Fort William Henry, situated on the southern shore of the lake, the 'dagger pointed at the heart of Canada'. The fort's garrison was massacred by the French Indians.

France's Indian allies, many of whom had previously been friendly, poured across the frontier, raiding, burning and scalping. Thousands of Americans were forced to flee from their western outposts. The *Pennsylvania Gazette* reported 'villages laid in ruins, men, women and children cruelly mangled and massacred'.

Murders, butcheries and scenes of horror were reported from New York to the Carolinas. Thousands of refugees poured into the coastal towns. The Governor of French Canada, de Vaudreuil, congratulated his Indian allies, believing 'there is no surer way to sicken the people of the English colonies of war and to make them desire the return of peace'.

Still the Colonists failed to unite for their mutual defence. The Pennsylvanians and Marylanders refused to renew the assault on Fort Duquesne; the New Yorkers thought only of defensive measures for their own safety. Colonial demoralization was complete. Everywhere the French were in the ascendant, their army continually reinforced by the transports which slipped through the British net. British preparations were, thought Governor Morris of Pennsylvania, proceeding 'as slowly as the enemy could desire'. The war, announced Thomas Pownall, Shirley's successor as Governor of Massachusetts, 'is no longer about a boundary, whether the French usurpation shall extend to this or that mountain, this or that river', but whether 'the French shall wrest from British hands the power of trade, whether they shall drive us out of this continent'. The *Boston Gazette* asked, 'If our colonies are ruined, where is our naval power? If our fleets become inferior, where is our dominion? And if our naval dominion is lost, Great Britain is no longer a free government, and the British Colonies no more a free people.'

In Parliament, Pitt criticised the conduct of the war on sea and land. 'We have provoked before we can defend', he told the House of Commons. In every quarter Britain had proved inferior to France. The succession of disasters shook the government. Unable to bear the weight of public resentment, the Duke of Newcastle sought to strengthen his ministry. There was no alternative to Pitt, but Pitt refused to serve under him. He demanded sole responsibility for the conduct of the war.

On Newcastle's inevitable resignation, announced on 11 November, Pitt joined forces with the youthful Duke of Devonshire to form a makeshift government. His position without a majority of votes was precarious but it enabled him to claim, 'I am sure that I can save the country and nobody else can'.

Could Pitt make good his boast?

National pride had been humiliated by the series of disasters. Britain's first duty was 'the succour and preservation of America', Pitt told Parliament on 3 December. He called for the creation of a national militia, the recruitment of Highland regiments (a bold move so soon after the Rebellion of 1745) and the increase of naval 41 strength. He would turn the tables on the French in North America, cut their sea artery, capture Louisbourg, the fortress on Cape Breton island, and carry the war into Canada by three-pronged invasions – up the St Lawrence, through Ticonderoga and Crown Point, and via the Great Lakes to capture Quebec. He told his friends of his great vision, his plan to conquer America by keeping the French occupied in Germany. Almost at once he was stricken by gout and confined to his bed. His magnetic voice was stilled. During his first short-lived ministry, Pitt could do no more than plan and exhort, galvanising the Colonists by his indomitable spirit. Privately, he admitted that the state of the nation was indeed perilous.

Pitt circulated his plans to the Colonial governors in America, promising reinforcements and requesting their Assemblies to raise troops at the Crown's expense. A squadron of battleships and eight thousand soldiers would be sent to Halifax in the spring. These reinforcements would raise British military strength in North America to seventeen thousand soldiers, treble the number of French regulars in Canada. He sent a squadron to the West Indies and another to India, risking depletion of the Home Fleet. It was essential, Pitt believed, to seize the command of the seas. The French fleet must be brought to battle or bottled up in its home ports by close blockade.

Pitt's plan for world conquest looked like foundering in Germany. Frederick had easily overrun Saxony, incorporating its army into his own. Even so the Prussians were outnumbered three to one by the Austrians alone, and Frederick's early attempt to crush the Austrian armies failed. No longer could he achieve a lightning victory, his only real chance of success. The Austrians advanced on Prussia, a land devoid of natural defences. Louis XV despatched a hundred thousand soldiers to aid his ally; the Czarina sent sixty thousand Russians marching through Poland. A League of German Catholic Princes was formed to crush the Protestant upstart. Frederick seemed doomed to be crushed by sheer weight of numbers. He marched, counter-marched, fought battles, laid and raised sieges, advanced and retreated, putting up a magnificent fight against fearful odds. Again and again his superb generalship saved him from annihilation.

The French now thrust into Germany, threatening Hanover. Pitt was content to let the King's Electorate be overrun, to be redeemed later. But to advocate such an unpopular course of action would wreck his chances of gaining George's favour, without which he could not remain in office. The protection of Hanover, Pitt had often said, was an 'un-British' measure. He had not concealed his opinion that Hanover was a liability, but to keep the King's favour, he was forced to change his policy. Pitt agreed that Britain should pay for an 'Army of Observation', a wholly German force to be commanded by the Duke of Cumberland, for the protection of Hanover; and also agreed to subsidise Frederick at the rate of £200,000 a year.

At the end of the war, after he had left office, Pitt stated that Britain had conquered America in Germany, implying that Britain had subsidised German armies to fight France in Europe. But Britain had no need to contain France in Europe. Even if her soldiers had not been kept busy, France could still not have transported them overseas in face of British naval might. Nor could her soldiers have been turned into sailors. The lack of a sea-faring population proved France's fatal weakness. Pitt's cousin, George Grenville, put it thus: 'It had not been the German war but the want of seamen that disabled France from prosecuting the war in America and from invading England.'

The Duke of Newcastle, by recording Pitt's statement in 1758 that it was in North America that 'England and Europe are to be fought for', may give us the best clue to Pitt's policy.

Pitt agreed to Britain's continental involvement in order to please his patron, the King. His easy acquiescence failed to impress George II. Pitt's plan of world conquest was beyond the understanding of a ruler who ignored the world outside Europe. Pitt failed to overcome George's hostility, his long-standing dislike of the man who had dared to speak of his 'paltry' Electorate and who had made friends with his son. Pitt was dismissed on 5 April 1757, after only four months in office.

His fall from power did not worry Pitt, for he knew he was indispensable. He was the popular hero. The people showed their feelings by a 'rain of gold boxes', the tokens of City freedom. Pitt waited in quiet expectancy while the Duke of Newcastle struggled to form another government. The Duke dared not resume office without Pitt as a shield. He feared popular resentment, he knew his own inadequacy to conduct the war. Without Pitt his parliamentary majority was a mockery. Pitt refused to compromise. He demanded complete control of the war as Secretary of State. The Duke could keep his patronage, dole out his places, provide the majority without which Pitt could not govern. Finally Newcastle agreed to subordinate himself to Pitt. The King accepted in bad grace.

The Pitt-Newcastle coalition took office on 29 June 1757.

At last Pitt could call the war his own. ⊱───────

Chapter 3

Pitt
Takes Control

Pitt stated at the start of his ministry that he was determined 'to push with vigour an offensive war'. By this he meant the conquest of Canada. Every other objective was secondary, every other consideration subordinate. Britain possessed the manpower and financial resources to achieve the total defeat of France in North America. The navy would bottle up her fleet and stifle her trade. The French economy was stagnant, her government impotent, her King sensual and indolent. Looking back with hindsight, with knowledge of the war's victorious outcome, Pitt's great plan seems to have been easy of accomplishment, and the final victory inevitable. He never doubted his ability to carry his war to a successful conclusion. As the war progressed and the victories mounted, Pitt's authority became absolute. He held greater power than any minister has done since. He carried the people with him, gained the King's trust, dominated the House of Commons, and treated his colleagues like servants. They knew that only Pitt could control the war: without him they were lost. They respected but feared him.

Pitt's great imperial vision was not shared by his ministerial colleagues, the Whig politicians who had been forced to accept him to secure their positions of dominance. The Duke of Newcastle dismissed the conquest of Canada as 'the idlest of all imagination'. Pitt was 'chief minister' on sufferance, to be cast aside when the emergency was over, his victories to be bartered in the final haggle when the opponents became exhausted by the struggle. Pitt suffered from the obstinacy and intrigues of the frightened men who in the early days of his ministry hampered his efforts to win an empire for Britain. He needed to tread warily both with his colleagues and with the hostile King. As yet there were no victories to prove him right, to make him the dictator he subsequently became. As the victories mounted he became less accommodating, threatening his reluctant colleagues with impeachment if they failed in their duties. They quarrelled and sulked, but they did his 'business'.

Pitt became Secretary of State for the Southern Department, the office which gave him charge of all British dependencies and of diplomatic relations with France and Spain. The Earl of Holdernesse returned to the Secretaryship for the Northern Department, which he had held previously under Pitt and once before in 1751. He dealt with Prussia and the Northern European states. These two Secretaries were responsible for all acts of administration at home and abroad which were not concerned with finance, and thus combined the modern offices of Home, Foreign and Colonial

Opposite Frederick the Great leading the charge of the Dragoons at the Battle of Kolin in Bohemia.

45

affairs. These divisions were not as disruptive as it would appear, for Holdernesse was cowed by Pitt and did his 'business' effectively. As nominal Prime Minister the Duke of Newcastle became, according to the practice established since 1715, First Lord of the Treasury, the controller of finance and the dispenser of places and promotions. His abysmal ignorance of American affairs is expressed by his often quoted remark, upon being advised to fortify Annapolis, 'Annapolis, Annapolis – certainly we must fortify Annapolis – where is Annapolis?'

Yet the Duke was essential to Pitt. He provided the base, the vote of the Commons, at the cost of his personal fortune, which enabled Pitt to govern. Pitt and Newcastle got on surprisingly well. 'They jog along like man and wife,' observed Lord Chesterfield, 'that is, seldom agreeing, often quarrelling, but by mutual consent upon the whole not parting.' Horace Walpole found that 'Pitt *does* everything, the Duke of Newcastle *gives* everything. As long as they agree in this particular they may do what they will.'

Newcastle filled the Cabinet with Whig sympathisers and placemen, politicians as heedless as he of Britain's manifest destiny. Pitt's followers were rigidly limited; his brother-in-law, Lord Temple, even more arrogant than he and without his brains, became Lord Privy Seal: this was then, as now, a non-administrative post. His cousins James and George Grenville were given minor offices. The great seaman, Lord Anson, the senior admiral and circumnavigator in 1740–44, returned to the Admiralty as First Lord, where he supported Pitt ably. The army was not under civilian control. The King retained his royal prerogative, the right to command, to appoint generals and distribute troops, responsibilities which Pitt succeeded in eroding as the royally appointed senior generals proved their incapacity.

Pitt conducted his business with the aid of two under-secretaries and nine clerks, one of whom occupied the hereditary office of Decypherer of Despatches. As Secretary of State he drew an annual salary of £5,680, which was reduced by certain expenses to £3,000, by contemporary values a far greater sum than is enjoyed by his modern successors. Pitt, it is said, always attended his office wearing full dress, with tie-wig, and would never permit his under-secretaries to sit in his presence. He required absolute obedience and did not allow his staff to take decisions without his authority. He punished acts of carelessness by taking the blame himself, thus disgracing the culprit. No detail was too small for his attention. He issued orders to other departments of state and checked that they had been performed. He took endless

Lord Anson, the First Lord of the Admiralty – the famous circumnavigator who ably supported Pitt in his determination that the Royal Navy must conquer the seas.

trouble correcting orders and despatches until they expressed his exact meaning, in striking contrast to his successors twenty-five years later, who contributed to the loss of the American Colonies by their ambiguous and ill-expressed correspondence. To manage the business he conducted, Pitt instituted a memorandum system whereby all matters in hand were itemised in abstracts and every order and despatch was listed under appropriate headings. As a result, the position on any matter could be grasped at a glance. He took advice from experts in every field, city merchants, sea-captains who traded with or had visited far-away places, and he adopted Newcastle's excellent espionage system by which the letters 47 of foreign diplomats were intercepted and read, and spies reported. Pitt relied also on his knowledge, and the experience gained from his lifelong study of history and of French psychology and language. This enabled him shrewdly to guess his enemy's intentions.

Pitt worked with daemonic energy and infected others with his spirit; this was the greatest single cause of his success as a war minister. When an admiral told him a task was impossible, he replied, 'Sir, I walk on impossibilities,' displaying his crutches and gouty feet. He bullied his colleagues, instructing them, as his correspondence shows, to take 'the most uncommon diligence in this matter'. He was always ready to improvise. The Admiralty needed to send guns to Portsmouth, seventy miles from London by road, where they were urgently needed. Traditionally naval guns were always transported by sea, a journey requiring several days. Pitt, in bed and stricken with gout, was told that the fleet's departure would be delayed. He enquired whether the Lords of the Admiralty had thought of sending the guns by road. He then organised a horse express, and the guns were delivered within twenty-four hours. On another occasion, when a general called to take his leave before going abroad, Pitt asked 'Have all your needs been supplied?'. There were many deficiencies, he was told. Pitt immediately dictated letters to the several departments concerned, and when the general sailed next day everything was ready.

Pitt left political favours to be dispensed by Newcastle, who lavished bishoprics, prebendaryships, tide-waiter-ships, Garters and Ribbons upon his supporters. Pitt, in contrast, sought and rewarded merit, offering no more than his thanks and those of the nation. Admiral Rodney volunteered for an irksome duty in order 'to contribute something to make his (Pitt's) administration what I sincerely wish it to be', and Wolfe disregarded his miserable health to serve him. Clive revered Pitt as the master-spirit of the war. No man, declared his one-time critic Isaac Barré, who had stood with Wolfe on the Plains of Abraham, ever entered his office 'who did not feel himself, if possible, braver at his return than when he went in'.

Pitt gained the devotion of the men he trusted and the affection of the people. He animated his officers with his burning zeal and took the people into his confidence, opening each session of Parliament with a broad statement of policy. He made the British people and the American Colonists, who to him were one people, feel that a fresh wind was blowing, that they were in the ascendant, that the war would make Britain rich and powerful. He infected others with his own enthusiasm. Yet according to his contemporaries he was arrogant, irritable, disdainful, inspiring fear, resentment and hatred amongst those whom he offended and thwarted in their ambitions. He made many enemies, including the King, who only modified his opinion of Pitt during the last year of his life. George failed to see that Pitt's 'business' was his own, despite its threat to his beloved Electorate.

Tactless and despotic Pitt may have been, but he was always careful to explain to his colleagues the reasons for his decisions. He sent them drafts of his proposals and called them to frequent meetings, often at their inconvenience. For his absence from one such meeting, the Duke of Newcastle pleaded the excuse that he was entertaining a Bishop at his house in the country. Pitt replied that he had hoped for the Duke's counsel 'concerning so important and extensive a scene as the campaign in America, where England and Europe are to be fought for'. He did not see his way as clear as he could wish, but 'I cannot, however, after the desire your Grace has expressed not to break the engagement at Claremont, press any further'. On another occasion Pitt, who was confined to his bed with gout, sent for the Duke who found him lying in an unheated room. Finding the cold unbearable, he crept into the spare bed. The two statesmen talked and gesticulated from beneath the bedclothes.

Pitt's great power lay in his foresight. He planned meticulously, issuing far-sighted orders, instructions to be carried out by men three thousand miles away, and isolated by six months' delay in communication. He needed to co-ordinate several campaigns or expeditions at once, and await their outcome. He never lost his grip. He concentrated on a vigorous offensive overseas, a rigid defensive policy at home. He never lost sight of his basic strategy. He believed in waging an offensive war, for that was the true strategy of defence.

Despite his frequent attacks of gout, during his four and a half years of power Pitt was free of mental breakdown. Never before or after did he enjoy twelve months' respite from bad health. Stimulated by his work, and his absolute belief that he alone could save England, Pitt set out to forge the army, navy and diplomacy into the blade of a single weapon. It took a year before he was ready to strike.

'A gloomy scene for this distressed, disgraced country.' That is how Pitt described the state of affairs when he took office on

29 June 1757. The country had been without a government since 6 April. In his short-lived earlier ministry Pitt had been able only to make plans for the future, rather than influence the course of events. The two wars in North America and Europe had become merged into one world-wide struggle which would decide the future of the British Empire and the European balance of power. In Europe, Hanover seemed defenceless, Prussia doomed to defeat.

On 18 June Frederick lost half his army, thirty thousand of his soldiers and his two best generals, in the frightful slaughter at Kolin in Bohemia, and much of the territory from which he drew men and money. The victorious Austrians poured into Silesia and even raided and plundered Berlin. A Russian army, a hundred thousand strong, massed on the frontier and the Swedes invaded Pomerania. On 26 July the Duke of Cumberland, commanding forty thousand German soldiers, was defeated at Hastenbach and forced to retire across the Weser, leaving Hanover wide open to French invasion. He capitulated at Klosteřzeven on 8 September, promising that his troops would not serve again for a year. King George repudiated his son's action.

The Earl of Chesterfield thought it evident that 'neither we, nor our ally the King of Prussia, can carry it on for three months longer'. The Lord Chancellor, the Earl of Hardwicke, found the situation abroad 'as bad as possible' and he trembled for the news that might come.

The French occupation of Hanover, Hesse and Brunswick did not particularly worry Pitt, except for its demoralising effect on the King. The possible and likely defeat of Prussia was more serious, for it would leave Britain to cope with France alone, with the invasion threat enhanced by the Austrian hand-over to her ally of the Channel ports of Nieuport, Ostend and Bruges. The French sent forty battalions to camp on the Belgian coast.

Pitt sought to relieve the pressure on Frederick by creating a powerful diversion on the French coast, in order to force the French to retain troops there, and at the same time to strike a heavy blow at France's naval construction. Pitt selected for the attack the port and naval base of Rochefort in the Bay of Biscay; it was to be a combined operation by navy and army. Every obstacle was placed in his way. The admirals and generals reported unfavourably on the project. They and the King wrangled over commanders, rejecting Pitt's plea for the selection of young and dashing officers. To command the military contingent George appointed Sir John Mordaunt, aged sixty and full of apprehension 'that the intended expedition may be hazardous in the greatest

Sir Eyre Coote, the
victor of Wandiwash.
Attributed to H. Morland

degree'. Pitt succeeded in getting a younger man, James Wolfe, appointed Quarter-Master-General. Admiral Hawke, the naval commander, appeared loath to set out and did so only under pressure from Pitt. On the arrival of his sixteen ships of the line and fifty-five transports at the mouth of the Charente, Hawke said he would land the troops wherever they were wanted, but showed little enthusiasm for the venture. Wolfe went ashore and returned with a plan to land between the island of Rhé and La Rochelle. At midnight on 27 September the soldiers were put in boats. Mordaunt then changed his mind and they were taken aboard again. Wolfe remarked that the troops 'were not allowed to attack the place they were ordered to attack, and for reasons no soldier will allow to be sufficient'. By 7 October the expedition was back at Spithead, with nothing accomplished.

The failure to raid Rochefort, which as was subsequently reported by spies would have fallen easily, was a terrible blow to Pitt. He vented his chagrin and disappointment on his colleagues.

The expedition's lamentable failure, combined with the Duke of Cumberland's ignominious capitulation, had two good effects. The threat to their ports forced the French to retain troops at home, thus reducing the pressure on Frederick. The British military failures

The Austrian Dragoons' charge at the Battle of Kolin, which totally defeated the Prussians, commanded by Frederick the Great.

Opposite page
Shah Alam conveying the government of Bengal to Clive. *From the painting by Benjamin West*

53

William Augustus, Duke of Cumberland, who capitulated with his army at Klosterzeven in Hanover leaving the way open for French invasion of the British King's German domain.

enabled Pitt to wrest military control from the King. Cumberland, in face of his father's fury, resigned his command, and Pitt obtained the promotion of Lord Ligonier to the rank of Field-Marshal with the function, if not the name, of Captain-General of the army, a post which brought him into the Cabinet as an adviser. Pitt was confident that Ligonier would do his 'business'.

King George was also in trouble with Frederick who, smarting from his loss of prestige, castigated his uncle as the cause of his misfortune. 'I would never have broken my alliance with France, but for your fair promises', he wrote in an indignant letter. Although he replied pleasantly, George was anxious for peace, hoping to preserve his Electorate from disaster. To keep the King happy, Pitt was forced to fortify Frederick with further subsidies to keep him in the war. But he steadfastly refused to send a fleet to the Baltic, as Frederick demanded, or commit British troops to fight on the Continent. Neither, as he picturesquely explained to the House of Commons, would he 'spend a drop of our blood to the Elbe, to be lost in that ocean of gore'. The huge sum of £670,000 was granted to Frederick, and the two kings signed a treaty covenanting 'that neither of the contracting powers shall conclude any peace, make any truce, or enter into any treaty of neutrality, of what kind soever, without the participation of the other'. Further grants were made to Hanover and Hesse totalling two million pounds, a stupendous sum in those days.

Suddenly and unexpectedly Frederick won two great battles, at Rossbach on 5 November and at Leuthen on 5 December, showing in both cases his superb military genius. At Rossbach he defeated a numerically superior Austro-French army and at Leuthen he crushed another far stronger Austrian army. The Russians and Swedes withdrew across the Prussian frontier; the French retreated to the Rhine.

'Heaven be praised for this great event. And now to our dinner with better appetite', remarked Pitt when he was told the news of Rossbach. He wrote to the victor, asking him to look at the whole field of war, not just Europe. Britain and Prussia were inevitably drawn together, their fortunes interwoven. The operations in Germany would assist the campaigns in America, and it was no less true that 'the war in America will contribute considerably to bring France to reason'. It was Pitt's first direct contact with Frederick, who blustered a little but agreed with Pitt's views. Pitt laboured at the despatch for five hours with Holdernesse, who complained that Pitt had been 'weighing words more than matter', and so mutilating the draft 'as to be scarcely legible'. Privately, Holdernesse admitted that it had been improved.

Worn with fatigue and 'broken-hearted' at the nation's condition, Pitt remained at his post over Christmas. He utterly despaired of better days, as he wrote privately to his cousin John Pitt whom he dreamed to be enjoying 'the solitude of verdant Dorsetshire, amidst warm leases, heavy ewes and bounding lambs'.

Good news was on the way. That 'Heaven Born General', as Pitt came to describe Robert Clive, had won a great victory in India. The tide was turning, the nightmare was nearly over. The years of defeat would soon give way to the years of victory.

Chapter 4

That Heaven Born General

The fusillade at Great Meadows on the American frontier ended the uneasy truce in India between the British and French trading companies, the free enterprise East India Company and the government-controlled Compagnie des Indes. The French had already missed their opportunity in India, due to their government's lack of perception and ignorance of local conditions. Their governor-general Dupleix had explained the guiding principles as early as 1740. Any small efficient European force could defeat any number of native troops, though these native troops could be welded into an effective army under European leadership. The Company could not win trade without gaining political control of the numerous corrupt states into which India was divided. These principles, later adopted by Clive, were rejected by the directors of the French company. 'We do not need states, but some ports for trade', they told Dupleix. They recalled him in 1754, instructing his successor, General Lally, to share the Indian trade with the British. The East India Company had foreseen the dangers of Dupleix's policy and had persuaded the French government that it was only Dupleix's wild ambitions which prevented the two companies from prospering in peaceful co-existence.

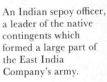

An Indian sepoy officer, a leader of the native contingents which formed a large part of the East India Company's army.

A Bengal sepoy Grenadier in the uniform of the East India Company.

Opposite Robert Clive, the conqueror of Bengal, receiving a contribution from the new ruler to the fund for disabled officers and soldiers.

57

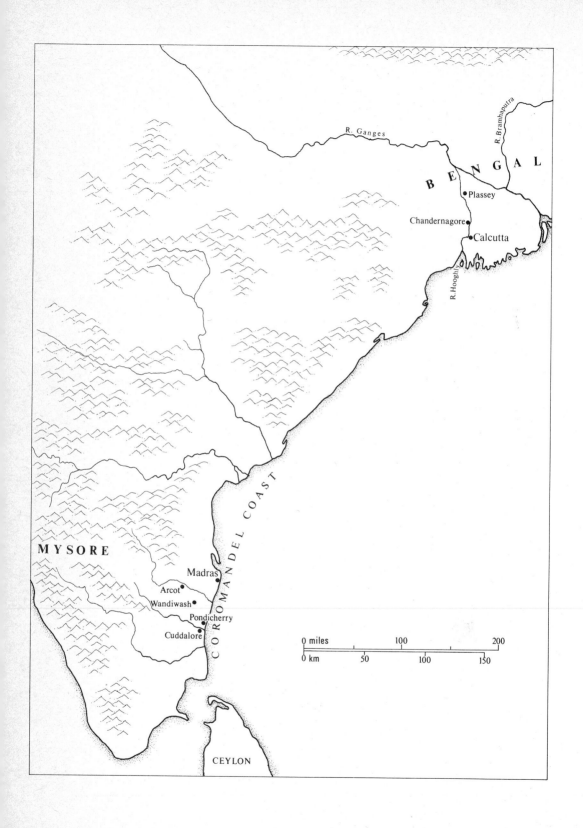

R. Ganges

R. Bramhaputra

B E N G A L

●Plassey

Chandernagore●

●Calcutta

R. Hooghly

C O R O M A N D E L   C O A S T

MYSORE

Madras●

Arcot●

Wandiwash●

Pondicherry●

Cuddalore●

CEYLON

0 miles   100   200
0 km   50   100   150

Dupleix's departure left India open to British aggression and to the aggrandisement of his great rival, Robert Clive. He profited from the dissensions and jealousies of the native rulers, the successors of the Great Mogul whose empire was breaking up.

The British had established themselves in Bengal, the French on the Coromandel coast and in the Carnatic, along the western shores of the Bay of Bengal. The British were based in Calcutta, Madras and Bombay, the French in Pondicherry. They also held Chandernagore on the Hooghly river above Calcutta.

Clive came to India as a clerk in the employ of the East India Company, a position he forsook for that of a company soldier, the commander of one of its native regiments. He won his great victories with little help from Britain. Pitt was content to leave India to Clive, and made no claim to share his achievements.

Pitt had no responsibility for Indian affairs, which were the concern of a private trading company. But he understood the importance of India 'where our strength lay', due to his family association with the sub-continent. His grandfather, Thomas Pitt, had been a famous freebooter and adventurer who had risen to the governorship of Madras and had amassed a great fortune.

Pitt's contribution to British victory in India was indirect. He found the ships with which to reinforce the fleet in the Indian ocean, with the result that Britain achieved naval dominance, denying the French access to their ports and preventing the reinforcement of their garrisons.

Above The Old Fort William, Calcutta, 1754, taken by the Bengalis and recaptured by Robert Clive at the start of the war.

Opposite:
The campaign in India 1754–1763. Following Robert Clive's conquest of Bengal, Colonel Eyre Coote defeated the French in Mysore, culminating in his great victory at Wandiwash.

59

Above The mentally deranged Suraj Dowlah who confined the luckless servants of the East India Company in the infamous **Black Hole** of Calcutta, and who was later vanquished by Clive at Plassey.

Above right The site of the Black Hole of Calcutta, the ancient prison in which 123 victims died.

The events that led to the destruction of French power in India began in 1756 with the accession to the throne of Bengal of Suraj Dowlah, aged twenty-three. The new Nabob was unstable, possibly demented, and treacherous. Ignoring the ancient treaty with the East India Company, he marched on Calcutta, destroyed the British fort, took captive the Company's servants, and imprisoned them overnight in a dungeon, the famous 'Black Hole'. Clive sailed with Admiral Watson to avenge the insult. He recaptured Calcutta and marched in pursuit of the Nabob, seizing the French fort at Chandernagore on the way.

Left Robert Clive, supported by Admiral Watson, captures the French trading post at Chandernagore in Bengal.

Robert Clive leading his troops at the Battle of Plassey where he defeated the Bengalis.

Clive caught up with Suraj Dowlah on 23 June 1757 at Plassey, on a branch of the Ganges. The Nabob commanded 40,000 horsemen, 60,000 foot soldiers, 50 elephants and 30 cannon which were served by French artillerymen. Clive had 700 British troops, 550 sailors brought by Admiral Watson, 1,700 native troops and 14 guns. He thought so little of his chances that he told an officer 'We must make the best fight we can during the day, and at night, sling our muskets over our shoulders and march back to Calcutta'. The Bengalis left their entrenched camp and, in the words of an anonymous diarist, 'approached apace, covering a fine extensive plain in front of us as far as the eye could discern from right to left'.

Opposite Robert Clive at the Battle of Plassey, standing on the roof of the Nawab's hunting lodge to survey the enemy lines.

Overleaf The British-owned port of Bombay, their naval base in Indian waters.

Clive advanced his British soldiers to an eminence within three hundred yards of the native camp. His guns far outranged the Nabob's, and threw back the charge of his horsemen. A sudden downpour wetted the enemy's powder, and the Bengalis fled in panic. The British lost seven men killed and thirteen wounded. Clive subsequently installed a puppet ruler in place of Suraj Dowlah, who was murdered by his own people.

Clive's famous, though easily won, victory placed the East India Company in undisputed control of Bengal. It possessed an even greater asset outside Bengal, a deep-water harbour at Bombay for

which the French had no counterpart. The French were forced to base their fleet across the Indian Ocean at the islands of Reunion and Mauritius. Their inability to refit in Indian waters made the French admirals over-cautious, more anxious to save their ships from damage than to fight decisive battles. As elsewhere, British sea-power contributed to the conquest of India. In answer to the East India Company's requests, Pitt sent four ships of the line to reinforce Watson's squadron of three warships: on Watson's death, Rear-Admiral George Pocock succeeded to the command.

The French were militarily superior to the British in the Carnatic, as long as Clive remained in Bengal. In 1756 the French government had sent out a fleet of eight ships, commanded by Commodore d'Ache, and two thousand regular soldiers. Lally captured the British trading posts at Cuddalore, Fort St David and Arcot, and in December 1758 laid siege to Madras. Pocock failed to provoke d'Ache into a fight, but he forced Lally to abandon the siege of Madras.

Clive appealed to Pitt for help. He wrote on 21 February 1759:

The repeated supplies furnished by the French from home compared with the handful of men sent out to us afford a melancholy proof that our Company are not of themselves able to take the proper measures for the security of their settlements; and unless they be assisted by the Nation they must inevitably at last fall a sacrifice to the superior efforts of the French Company supported by their Monarch.

Clive thought that the French government might turn its arms towards India, 'in hopes of an equivalent for the losses they have reason to apprehend in America'.

In response to Clive's plea for help, Pitt despatched a regiment under the command of Colonel Eyre Coote, and two more warships. He did this in 1759, at the height of the invasion scare when his colleagues were clamouring for the recall of men and ships to prevent the expected French landings in Britain.

Pitt inadvertently decreased French strength in India. His plan

to send an expedition to capture Mauritius became known to the French government, which ordered d'Ache to take his fleet to protect the island. He sailed from Pondicherry, leaving Lally to his fate. D'Ache again avoided decisive battle with Pocock whose fleet of nine vessels was outnumbered by d'Ache's eleven ships. Lally concentrated on saving Pondicherry, believing, as he informed his government, that 'It was better to act in destroying the enemy than to expire from want', meaning that cut off from France by the British blockade, the French in India would soon be reduced by famine.

Lally advanced from Pondicherry and laid siege to the British fort at Wandiwash, sixty miles south-east of Madras. The fort held out for three months, giving time for Colonel Eyre Coote to march from Madras. The two armies were about equal in strength, each comprising regular soldiers and native contingents. Lally opened with his artillery, and believing it to have been effective, launched a cavalry charge. The horsemen were received with a blast of grapeshot and musket fire. Lally led his infantry in direct assault on the British line. A lucky British shell, which exploded the French powder magazine, imperilled the French left. Seeing the French marines retreat, Eyre Coote sent a regiment to turn their flank. Lally's front disintegrated and he retreated to Pondicherry, abandoning several of his most notable officers who were taken prisoner.

Following his decisive victory at Wandiwash, which ended French domination of southern India, Eyre Coote captured French settlements, isolating and laying siege to Pondicherry. For Lally one hope remained, that d'Ache would return to challenge the supremacy of the British fleet, now comprising sixteen ships commanded by Admiral Stevens who had taken over on Pocock's return to Britain.

Lally looked in vain for d'Ache. He had sailed to Mauritius in response to his government's order. With the city surrounded on sea and land by hostile forces, his soldiers reduced to starvation, Lally prepared to defend Pondicherry, believing it better, as he told Marshal Belle-Isle, the French War Minister, 'to die of steel than famine'.

Eyre Coote moved slowly, awaiting the end of the rainy season, to complete his investment of the last French fort. By 6 December he had established four batteries which shelled the town, while four British warships patrolled the roadstead. Lally had food to last for only three weeks. Providence came to his aid. On 1 January 1761 the Coromandel coast was struck by a hurricane. In the words of an eye-witness, 'along all the shores there was only the wreckage of vessels'. The British squadrons suffered severe damage, though thanks to their seamanship only four ships were lost. The military forces suffered more severely. 'The violence of the wind so engulfed the European soldiers that they could not move; a great many sepoys perished, the torrents formed by the rain overwhelmed their camp, the cannon for the most part were buried and the batteries had been also overthrown.'

The British cleared the debris and rebuilt their batteries. By 13 January eleven 24-pounders were playing upon Pondicherry.

Lally capitulated. The fall of their last outpost blasted French hopes of establishing a trading empire in India. India was destined to be British, thanks to British naval supremacy. The results were immediate. In 1754 the French East India Company had sent home goods valued at £1,000,000; by 1761 the British were exporting goods valued at £1,750,000; the French nothing.

The East India Company recognised Pitt's contribution to victory, owing 'not only their present glorious situation, but their very existence to his generous protection'. With Pitt's help, Clive, Eyre Coote and others had founded an Empire.

Chapter 5

Plans
for Victory

The North American campaigns in 1757 had ended in disaster and disappointment, though this was not Pitt's fault for he did not assume responsibility until June, by which time their fate had been decided. The French remained undisputed masters of Lakes Ontario, Champlain and George. During the summer season forty-three ships had evaded the British blockade, which was not yet fully organised, bringing to Canada thirty-five hundred reinforcements and munitions of war. Louisbourg, the fortress on Cape Breton island, remained in French possession. Pitt and his cabinet colleagues eagerly awaited news of its capture.

Following his arrival in America in 1756 Lord Loudon, the Commander-in-Chief, had been in two minds whether to attack Louisbourg or to bypass the fortress and assault Quebec. For the reduction of Louisbourg and the other enterprises Pitt, during his first ministry, had provided seventeen thousand soldiers and a powerful fleet. On 1 May 1757, Loudon received definite instructions to attack Louisbourg first, in order to deprive the French of their naval base, the only North Atlantic refuge for the French fleet.

Admiral Holburne, Pitt stated, would sail from Portsmouth in March, with fourteen ships of the line, convoying fifty transports carrying five thousand soldiers. He ordered Loudon to remain at New York until he learned of Holburne's arrival at Halifax, Nova Scotia. He was then to go there with his troops and ships which, with those from Britain, would bring his force to seventeen ships of the line and fourteen thousand soldiers. That should be sufficient to reduce Louisbourg, a task which had been accomplished in 1745 by a small force of Americans acting on their own.

The Atlantic storms frustrated Pitt's plan. Strong westerly winds which blew continuously for two months delayed Holburne's departure, and it was 8 May before he could clear the Isle of Wight. These gales favoured the French, by disrupting the blockade of the northern ports and helping ships from the southern ports to sail across the Atlantic and swing northwards to Cape Breton. Taking advantage of the weather and the storm-battered British blockading squadrons, eighteen French ships of the line, several of them more powerful than the vessels of Holburne's fleet, slipped out of harbour and sailed to Louisbourg, where they all arrived by 19 June.

This naval concentration greatly strengthened Louisbourg. Its batteries had been considerably augmented since 1749, when it was returned to French possession. Another factor operated in the

Opposite General Abercromby, who led his British troops to disaster at Fort Ticonderoga.

71

defenders' favour: persistent summer fogs obscured the harbour from prying eyes.

On hearing of Admiral Holburne's arrival at Halifax on 10 July, Loudon sailed from New York. Ten days later the naval and military officers conferred in Halifax, and the council agreed that the attack on Louisbourg should be launched. Embarkation of troops was delayed until information had been received about the strength and number of warships in the harbour. Frigate after frigate returned to report that Cape Breton island was shrouded in mist, and it was not until 5 August that another captain succeeded in penetrating the fog. He reported the presence of eighteen ships of the line. Loudon decided to postpone the assault to another year.

The news of the postponement of the enterprise, the most important operation of the campaign, exasperated Pitt. He blamed the over-cautious Loudon, whom he recalled to Britain. To replace him, the King insisted on the appointment of the second-in-command, fifty-two-year-old General James Abercromby. Pitt probably acquiesced in rather than approved of the promotion of a man who had shown himself timid and fearful. But Abercromby was the man on the spot and other senior officers were reluctant to serve in America, preferring to win their laurels in Europe where they understood the type of warfare. Having settled the matter of command, Pitt wrote to each Colonial Governor, and to Abercromby, explaining his plans for 1758. Their conception and magnitude can only be fully appreciated against the background of the time.

Britons rather than Frenchmen envisaged defeat in the war which was now moving into its third year. Pitt himself admitted that the state of the nation was 'indeed perilous'. Cynically, Horace Walpole thought it was 'time for England to slip her cables and float away into some unknown ocean'. It would be Britain's fate to perish without losing her fleet or her armies, believed a correspondent to the *London Magazine*. 'Every mail,' announced the editor of the *London Sentinel*, 'acquaints us of some new triumph of the enemy, the country is saddled with a debt of eighty millions, the interest of which we can hardly defray.' The news from Europe and America was equally black. Britain was making no headway against a formidable enemy. The *New York Gazette*, expressing Colonial opinion, described 1757 as 'a year of the most dishonour to the Crown, of the most detriment to the subject, and of the most disgrace to the nation'. In sum, Britain seemed impotent, unable to carry on the war, far less achieve victory.

72   The French in Canada were equally sombre, being beset by

difficulties. The harvest had failed for two years and the province was struck by famine. Food was so severely rationed that Montcalm thought 'the colony must perish for want of bread'. Lack of provisions would prevent further military action. Supplies from France had been cut drastically by the British blockade. Internal corruption and high taxation added to the distress. The Governor, de Vaudreuil, and the military commander, Montcalm, disliked and feared each other. Their rivalry and personal animosity resulted in bitter disputes as to how best to employ the Colony's meagre force of sixty-eight hundred regular soldiers. They were outnumbered three to one by the British. De Vaudreuil believed that the assault on Louisbourg had only been postponed. Montcalm thought that the next attack would come via the lakes.

Pitt was not unaware of Canada's economic plight, which had been disclosed by spies. He took no notice of the moaners, the fainthearted who saw a major disaster in every minor defeat or set-back. His actions, whether or not he fully understood their im-plications, show that he appreciated the fundamental fact that in war, if its strategy is sound, a nation can recover from tactical mistakes. But if strategy is unsound, tactical successes will not bring victory. The secret of success lay in concentrating a superior force in the right place. Britain could do this thanks to her over-whelming naval superiority, which enabled her to strike overseas and deny that power to the enemy.

Pitt announced his plans for 1758. To conquer Canada, Britain would raise fifty thousand soldiers and twenty thousand sailors. He invited the Colonial Governors and Assemblies to mobilise and equip twenty thousand of these men, their cost to be paid for by the Crown. He promised to supply arms, ammunition, tents and artillery trains. He took the Americans into his confidence, inviting them to join 'the Body of the King's Forces' for invading Canada, in order to 'avert the Dangers impending'. His Majesty had nothing more at heart, he told them, than 'to repair the Losses and disappointments of the last inactive, and unhappy campaign'. To General Abercromby he was more explicit, outlining and detailing the three separate campaigns to be undertaken, naming their officers, enumerating the detachments required and ordering the construction and collection of boats on the lakes.

Pitt overcame the Americans' reluctance to assist in the war fought for their protection. So far their response had been indifferent. Virginia for example had been able to raise only 424 men, from its paper-strength of 25,000 militiamen, to help Loudon. Pennsylvania had supplied 1,200 and New Jersey half that 73 number. The Assemblies of New York and Massachusetts, both nearer to the foe, had been more forthcoming, but their contingents had proved inefficient and prone to desertion. The southern colonies had been unco-operative; their planters and merchants were fully occupied making money from the war boom.

The modern American historian Lawrence Henry Gipson (*The Great War For Empire*) believes the American colonies possessed the potential strength, with little aid from the mother country, to drive the French from the advanced positions they had occupied. However, they lacked the resources and military experience to conquer Canada on their own. Their safety from French aggression depended upon British help.

Professor Gipson has been criticised by other American historians for over-emphasising the part played by Britain in the war which finally freed the Americans from the French threat. Gipson set out to rectify the myths created by historians who wrote soon after the Revolutionary War by which the Americans achieved their independence. In this war the rebellious colonists showed themselves to be doughty fighters, the match for the disciplined Redcoats, and far more experienced in frontier-type warfare. Conversely, they must have possessed and shown the same skills twenty-five years before. British motives in the earlier war had been, these historians declared, purely selfish. American propaganda then required them to paint the picture of the rapacious British Empire reaching out greedy hands from London to grasp everything in sight. The colonists in 1757 did not believe that. They understood Britain's concern for their welfare, but they lacked confidence in their own capabilities and suffered from certain indignities. Pitt, by an imaginative decision, removed their chief grievance, the subservience of their officers to those of the regular army, irrespective of rank. He gave American officers equal status by royal warrant, though not always with happy result, for few Americans had had the necessary experience in active combat at lower grades.

Professor Gipson pays glowing tribute to Pitt's contribution to victory:

It was to William Pitt, who through his superb leadership, his mobilisation of the manpower, the military and the financial resources of the mother country, and, finally, through his capacity to instil a spirit of co-operation, at least temporarily, and also of confidence, in the minds of the all too individualistic Americans, that the chief credit for supplying the answers to these questions must be given. Strange as it may seem, this perhaps greatest of all of their benefactors, the one above all others who guaranteed to them a great future on this continent, where they could dwell in security; this statesman who was willing to sacrifice almost every other consideration for the promotion of their future welfare – an attitude quite devoid of all sinister or cynical ulterior motives – this champion who supported them even in rebellion and believed in them in season and out, now as leader of His Majesty's government and then as leader of the opposition, was never properly recognised by Americans of his own generation or by their descendants. While monuments by the hundreds have been erected to lesser men here in the broad expanses of the United States, where is that monument, outside of the place named in his honour at the forks of the Ohio (Pittsburg) by those of the regular army and a few small towns and counties, which worthily expresses a sense of gratitude or, if not gratitude, at least a sense of some appreciation for his great services to the American people? When, indeed, will this people at length free itself of that hoary distortion of the plain facts of history that would make the war that is now being described, not one entered into by the mother country primarily for the purposes of protecting the vital interests of the American colonials, but rather just another episode in the history of an aggressive, rapacious, grasping, calculating British imperialism, as Thomas Paine saw it, and as Bancroft proclaimed it to be?

The Americans responded gladly to Pitt's call for unprecedented effort in 1758. The day before his message was received, the Massachusetts Assembly had reluctantly voted 2,000 men. Next day the quota was increased to 7,000. For the campaigns planned for the year the northern colonies recruited 17,500 men, while the more sparsely populated southern colonies contributed 5,300.

Pitt envisaged a triple offensive: against Louisbourg (and eventually Quebec); Montreal, via the Hudson river, Lakes George and Champlain and the Richelieu river; with a flanking movement via Lake Ontario and assault on Fort Duquesne. To the new Commander-in-Chief, Abercromby, he described it as 'this great, and it is hoped, decisive campaign'. At the same time Pitt despatched four fleets, one to the west coast of France, one to the Mediterranean to bottle up the French fleet and prevent reinforcements from reaching Canada, another to the West Indies to harass the French islands, and a fourth to India. Expeditions were also sent to raid the French ports of Cherbourg and St Malo, both nests of privateers, and to capture the French West African trading stations.

Pitt hoped to conquer Canada in one year.

Abercromby was charged with the conduct of the lakes campaign, the ascent of the Hudson river, the portage to Lake George, the crossing of that lake to Fort Ticonderoga, which protected the passage to Lake Champlain, and on to Crown Point and the Richelieu river. His objective was Montreal. Ticonderoga, or Fort Carillon as the French called it, was the most formidable obstacle likely to be encountered. To capture it quickly, it was essential, as Pitt had planned, to benefit from the earlier thawing of the Hudson which could be expected to be free of ice two weeks before the more northerly Richelieu river. The Canadian climate would delay the despatch of French troops to reinforce the fort's weak winter garrison. To gain this advantage, Abercromby needed to sail up lake George early in May. He might have been able to keep to that schedule had he not been hampered by Pitt's order to add twenty thousand Colonials to his force of sixty-three hundred British regulars. In this instance Pitt planned too precisely, embarrassing his field commander with unnecessary Colonial levies. Their recruitment was not completed until the end of June, and by then only six thousand had reached Lake George. Their late mobilisation was due to the tardy arrival of the vessels carrying their arms. These ships left England on 19 February and did not reach New York until 14 June. From Massachusetts came 2,853 men, from Connecticut 475, from New York 1,715, and from New Jersey 922. They were mostly untrained levies, some of them deserters from the previous campaign who had been pardoned by Abercromby. He had little faith in their fighting qualities. Nor was the expected Indian support forthcoming. Sir William Johnson had lost his influence with the Six Nations, who in his words were torn between the 'French and English faction'. He could produce only 395 braves, and then too late to be of use.

Abercromby proved an unfortunate choice as field-commander. Though kindly and tactful, he lacked spirit and aggressiveness. He had served against the French in Flanders during the previous war, that of the Austrian Succession, but had never held independent command. Abercromby's lack of capability was offset by Pitt's choice of Lord Howe as brigadier, 'the best officer in the British army' as Wolfe called him. Aged thirty-four, George Augustus Howe, one of the several brothers of that name, was an outstanding personality, loved and respected by his own soldiers and by the Colonials.

The army assembled at the site of Fort William Henry on the southern shore of Lake George, where a thousand bateaux and ninety whale-boats had been collected. The soldiers embarked on 4 July and the armada set out, making an impressive sight, covering the lake from side to side and extending from front to rear for a full seven miles. Some of the soldiers, both Colonials and British,

carried the 'Kentucky Rifle', the frontiersmen's precision weapon which had caught the fancy of a British officer. He had taken one home and it was manufactured for the army, although in limited numbers. This innovation failed to take root. It was the Americans rather than the British who used this rifle to devastating effect in the Revolutionary War.

General Montcalm celebrates with his troops following the defeat of the British assault on Fort Ticonderoga, 1758.

Montcalm reached Ticonderoga at the end of June. The winter in Canada had been particularly severe, delaying the assembly and transportation of troops, as did the continued shortage of provisions. Thirteen merchantmen reached Quebec in mid-June, bringing food 'though very trifling in comparison with the vastness of our wants', as one officer wrote. Montcalm brought five thousand soldiers to strengthen Ticonderoga's garrison of a thousand men.

Fort 'Ty', as the Americans affectionately called it, is now a place of pilgrimage, due largely to the importance it gained in the Revolutionary War, when it fell to the British who came from the north. But the earlier battle is not forgotten, for as I saw in 1967,

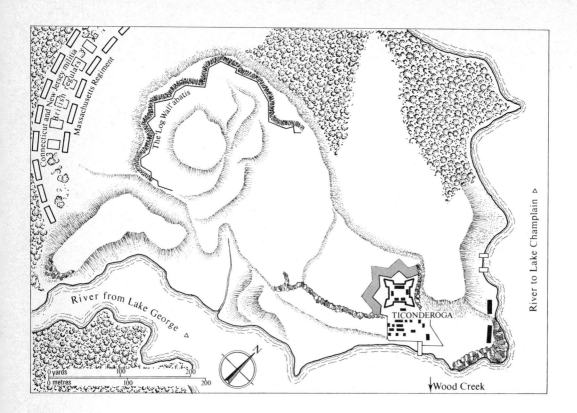

On the map:
Connecticut and New Jersey militia
British regulars
Massachusetts Regiment
The Log Wall 'abatis
River from Lake George
River to Lake Champlain
TICONDEROGA
Wood Creek
0 yards 100 200
0 metres 100 200

Fort Ticonderoga at the confluence of Lakes Champlain and George, which is now upper New York State. The British failed to capture the fort in 1758; a year later it fell without a blow.

the 'Old French Lines', the outer defences raised and defended by Montcalm, have been recreated as mute testimony to the tragic fate of the Black Watch and of the 464 Britons who died there. The star-shaped stone fort stands near the tip of a rocky promontory, flanked by Lake Champlain on the north and Wood Creek to the south. This creek is connected to Lake George, further to the west, by a stream which required a portage over rapids, and by a waggon-road. The fort itself is dominated by the sugar loaf hill, subsequently named Mount Defiance, from the height of which in 1777 the British artillery rendered Ticonderoga untenable. Montcalm thought little of the fort's chances of withstanding attack. He concentrated his forces at the head of Lake George, the only feasible approach for an army following that route. His scouts reported the approach of an immense fleet, carrying an army estimated to number twenty thousand men.

The British landed on 6 July on the west bank of the lake, the soldiers swarming ashore without opposition. They formed into four columns with the intention of marching round the head of the lake, to take Ticonderoga in the rear. The advance guard, led by Howe, marched into a French detachment sheltering in thick

78

woods. He fell mortally wounded at the first shot, to the grief of his men and the sorrow of his friends. A year later the Massachusetts Assembly subscribed the large sum of £250 to pay for the erection of a memorial in Westminster Abbey. Howe's fall demoralised the army. The naval Captain Loring, who had been placed by Pitt in charge of the boats, wrote 'So far things had been properly conducted, and with spirit'. But no sooner was Howe dead 'than everything took a different turn and ended in confusion and disgrace'.

The French fell back upon the fort's outer defences, and next day the British cautiously advanced to within one mile. A junior officer, due to the indisposition of the Chief Engineer, was sent forward to reconnoitre the fort's defences. He returned to report that they were weak and could be carried by frontal attack, dangerous advice which Abercromby failed to check for himself.

Abercromby had the choice of three possibilities; to besiege the fort and starve its garrison into surrender; to blast it into submission; or to assault it by direct frontal attack. Basing his decision on the unreliable report of the young officer, and in the erroneous belief that six thousand French reinforcements were on their way, Abercromby elected to assault, leaving his artillery at the landing place, whereas a few hours' pounding would have destroyed the fort's log-wood defences. Had he gone forward, he might have noticed, as did Captain Loring, the 'ally' offered by the sugar loaf hill, from the height of which the fort could be dominated, as the French themselves feared.

About a cannon-shot's distance from the fort Montcalm erected an abatis, the 'Log Wall' as it is called, constructed of the intertwined trunks of trees and branches, seven to eight feet high, projecting outward and zig-zagging across the neck of the promontory. It was manned by three thousand regulars. The cannon were mounted on the ramparts of the fort. That night Montcalm did receive some reinforcements, four hundred regulars led by Brigadier Lévis. Even so the French were in peril, outnumbered three to one and with provisions sufficient for only five days.

Having apparently lost his wits, Abercromby drew up his infantry in line of battle. The light infantry, various boatmen and rangers formed an advance skirmishing line, ahead of the Massachusetts regiment. The British regulars who would carry the burden of assault, marched next. The Connecticut and New Jersey militia were held in reserve. Abercromby gave orders that the attacking troops were 'to march briskly, rush upon the enemy's fire and not to give theirs until they were within the enemy's breastwork'. 79

The battle began at half-past twelve o'clock. The British right, and then the centre, moved forward in long lines, three deep. The soldiers quickly became snarled in the abatis, unable to advance or retreat, but breaching the order not to fire. The 42nd Highlanders, the Black Watch, attempted to hack their way

through the fallen trees with their broadswords. Dried by the hot July sun, the interwoven branches caught fire, an eventuality for which Montcalm had prepared; bucket parties brought water from the river. Several Highlanders broke through the breastwork; their Commander, Duncan Campbell, fell mortally wounded.

The Black Watch became enmeshed in the 'Log Wall' guarding Fort Ticonderoga.

Robert Louis Stevenson immortalised Campbell's end in his poem about Inverawe Castle, of which Campbell was the Laird. In his youth, in the early seventeen-forties, a ghost appeared to him in a dream, and in bidding him farewell told him they would meet again at Ticonderoga, a name that then meant nothing to Campbell. The ghost reappeared the night before the battle. Campbell awakened to learn that he would lead the assault on the fort named in his dream.

At sunset Abercromby withdrew his men to the landing place. The Black Watch had lost 203 men killed and 296 wounded. The British casualties amounted to 1,610 regulars and 334 Colonials, killed and wounded. The French losses were small in comparison, 106 killed and 266 wounded: Montcalm was astonished at the ease with which the assault had been beaten back. Abercromby blamed his Colonial militia. Some, he told Pitt, deserted or shammed sick, and the officers, with few exceptions, were worse than the men. Others behaved with great credit, particularly the Massachusetts and Connecticut troops. Abercromby's mishandling of the attack at Ticonderoga, following Braddock's disaster, increased American mistrust of British battle tactics.

The British advance on Montreal had been stopped dead. Abercromby took his army back to the southern end of Lake George, where he was asked by Lieutenant-Colonel John Bradstreet to entrust him with thirty-six hundred Colonials for the attack on Fort Frontenac on Lake Ontario. A native of Maine, Bradstreet was, in James Wolfe's opinion, a 'most remarkable man'. He had fought at Louisbourg in 1745 and had been rewarded with a regular commission, achieving command of the Royal American Regiment in 1757. He was just the man to lead the expedition against Frontenac, a project he had long advocated and for which he had offered to raise a force at his own expense. Bradstreet's offer pleased Pitt so much that he proposed to promote the enterprising officer as Quarter-Master-General of the army in the Southern Colonies, a commission which Abercromby rescinded. He needed the enterprising Bradstreet to organise the boat-building on Lake George. But later searching desperately for some success to offset his humiliating failure at Ticonderoga, Abercromby was persuaded to agree to Bradstreet's proposal.

Bradstreet pushed up the Mohawk river, embarked his men on Lake Ontario and reached Fort Frontenac on 26 August, having covered a distance of 430 miles which required 84 miles of portages. The garrison of 110 soldiers was taken completely by surprise and surrendered. The loss of the fort on Lake Ontario was

George Augustus Howe, the 'best officer in the British army,' as Wolfe described him, who was killed before Fort Ticonderoga.

serious, Montcalm believed, for it cut the French frontier line in two. Bradstreet's bloodless victory severed the French supply line to Fort Duquesne on the Ohio. Provisions and reinforcements were sorely needed there. Nonetheless, Montcalm did not think that the British would attack the Ohio.

Brigadier-General John Forbes was in fact already on his way to assault Duquesne, the fort built by the French at the forks of the Ohio to prevent American westward expansion, and which Braddock had failed to capture.

Pitt had chosen the right man for the arduous task of raising and transporting an army of seven thousand men and a train of artillery through the trackless wilderness. This could be done, Forbes believed, only by methodical, slow advance, by making roads and establishing supply depots every forty miles. 'By

83

GENERAL JOHN FORBES (1710-1759)

Brigadier-General John Forbes who led the successful attack on Fort Duquesne, which he renamed 'Pittsburg' in honour of William Pitt.

which means,' he told Pitt, 'although I advance but gradually, yet I still go more surely.' Forbes, a Scotsman born in 1707, had experienced active service in Flanders and had fought at Culloden, the graveyard of the Young Pretender's hopes. He had risen steadily in rank, but when in 1757 he was promoted to Brigadier-General, he had the galling experience of finding himself placed below his junior, Jeffrey Amherst.

Forbes came to Philadelphia in April, faced with the difficult task of raising five thousand militia to strengthen his army of seventeen hundred regulars. The southern colonies, he reported sadly, were disinclined to bestir themselves. Their Assemblies voted men but debated their cost. Fresh disputes arose every day. By late June only forty-five hundred men had assembled. With few exceptions, Forbes told Pitt, the officers were 'an extremely bad collection of broken inn-keepers, horse jockeys and Indian traders'. The men were 'a gathering of the scum of the worst of people'.

84

Forbes tended to revise his opinion later, commending 'to do justice' the spirit of some of these levies whom he found had 'but one blanket each, which will not do in these cold evenings and mornings, no shoes, stockings or breeches'.

Six hundred Cherokee Indians came to Philadelphia, 'almost naked and without arms'. All but fifty deserted due to 'their natural fickle disposition which is not to be got the better of by fair words or presents, of both of which they have had a great deal'.

Six thousand waggons and teams were collected, the farmers supplying their worst horses and most rickety waggons at the rent of fifteen shillings a day.

Rejecting the advice of Washington, now Brigadier-General in command of the Virginian contingent, to follow Braddock's road, Forbes elected to take the more direct but harder route from Pennsylvania, which required the penetration of an immense forest and the crossing of several mountain ranges. It was fortunate that he so chose because the French expected him to take the old road. They spent their energies in securing passes and fords over the river where Braddock had died.

The army reached Carlisle, the frontier settlement of Pennsylvania, 120 miles west of Philadelphia, on 10 July. Ahead lay 'an immense, uninhabited wilderness, overgrown everywhere with trees and underbrush, so that no where can anyone see twenty yards'. Forbes feared that he might fail to reach his objective before the winter rains put an end to his advance. On 6 September the army was still forty miles from Fort Duquesne. Forbes sent Major James Grant ahead with 838 picked men. They were ambushed and lost three hundred of their number. Moving slowly and cautiously, Forbes reached the environs of the fort on 26 November. Ahead he heard the sound of explosions. Desperately short of provisions, the garrison had destroyed and abandoned their fort.

Next day Forbes wrote to Pitt. 'I have used the freedom,' he told him, 'of giving your name to Fort Duquesne, as I hope it was in some measure the being actuated by your spirit that now makes us masters of the place.' He headed his letter 'Pittsburg'.

Leaving a garrison to hold the ruined fort, Forbes returned to Philadelphia. He died there in March, a few weeks before the arrival of Pitt's letter congratulating him on his great achievement and thanking him for 'the undeserved honour you have done my name'.

Montcalm, when he learned of the fort's fall, called it the 'branch that exhausts the trunk'. He had greater worries than the loss of the Ohio.

Chapter 6

Louisbourg
and Guadeloupe

The assault on Louisbourg was the most important operation of the campaign, for its capture would cut the province's supply line and provide a jumping-off place for the attack on Quebec, which Pitt hoped would be launched in 1758. For the siege of Louisbourg, he provided the maximum effort, the best soldiers and the most energetic commanders. To command the army Pitt chose forty-one-year-old Jeffrey Amherst and promoted him from Colonel to Major-General, over the heads of the senior officers favoured by the King. Amherst had been in the army for twenty-three years, had fought at Dettingen and Fontenoy, in the war of the Austrian Succession, and had served in Germany with the Duke of Cumberland. He had shown himself to be a capable, steady, if not brilliant officer. When the King objected to Amherst's youth, Pitt refused to change his mind, saying that he would rather abandon the attack on Louisbourg. To offset Amherst's caution Pitt provided three energetic brigadiers, Wolfe, Whitmore and Lawrence. The latter had served in Louisbourg during the short British occupation following its capture by the New Englanders in 1745, and knew its strengths and weaknesses. To accomplish his difficult task Pitt gave Amherst an army of 13,200 men, mostly British regulars, and a great artillery train.

To command the fleet Pitt selected Admiral Edward Boscawen, who knew the North American waters, giving him twenty-one battleships and fourteen frigates. Eight of these ships of the line were already at Halifax where they had wintered following the previous campaign. Boscawen sailed from Plymouth on 23 February, in ample time, Pitt hoped, to complete the reduction of Louisbourg by the end of June. Should that feat be accomplished, Amherst and Boscawen were ordered to sail up the St Lawrence and besiege Quebec where, Pitt also hoped, they would be met by the victorious Abercromby.

Pitt was over-optimistic. Boscawen's ships encountered, as Wolfe described, the opposition of contrary winds, calms and currents, and did not reach Halifax until 9 May. Amherst, sailing in the *Dublin* with Captain Rodney, was further delayed by that officer's insistence on chasing a rich French merchantman whose capture occupied fourteen days. The whole fleet, including the transports, assembled in Halifax harbour on 24 May.

Wolfe voiced his impatience and his dissatisfaction. The troops were too few for the great enterprise, their muskets were in poor condition, the soldiers' clothes were unsuitable for the climate,

Opposite The Royal Navy capture and destroy one of the French warships guarding Louisbourg harbour. This night attack opened the way for a fine military assault on the fortress.

87

General Jeffrey
Amherst, the British
Commander-in-Chief in
North America during
the victorious years.

they were ruined by their constant diet of salt-meat and rum, and had too much money. He formed a poor opinion of the Colonial levies. 'The Americans are in general the dirtiest, most contemptible cowardly dogs that you can conceive. There is no depending upon them in action. They fall down dead in their own dirt and desert by battalions, officers and all. Such rascals as those are rather an incumbrance than any real strength to an army.'

The fleet left Halifax on 29 May and reached Louisbourg on 2 June. The strength of the fortress lay in its position on a storm-bound, fog-infested, rocky coast. The town, which had been founded in 1713, lay at the spit of a rugged promontory which enclosed the spacious harbour. Its narrow entrance was protected by two fortified islands. Guarded by even two warships the harbour was inaccessible to a hostile fleet, and the French had managed to get five ships of the line into Louisbourg.

The Atlantic weather had once again defeated Pitt's plans. He had taken care to prevent the French from concentrating a superior fleet at Louisbourg as they had done in the previous year. At the close of the season Admiral de la Motte had taken his ships to France, losing two thousand sailors on the voyage from plague and carrying the disease into Brest.

Pitt had intended that Boscawen should reach Louisbourg as soon as that port was ice-free, to forestall any French ships which might evade the blockade of their coasts. Admiral Hawke succeeded in paralysing the French preparations in the Bay of Biscay; Commodore Osborne turned back the French Mediterranean squadron at Gibraltar with the loss of two of its largest ships. De la Motte, his ships short of seamen and the town in its death-throes, was unable to leave Brest. Rochefort was perforce left unguarded. Admiral des Gouttes slipped out with five warships and eight other vessels, reaching Louisbourg in April. He carried supplies and reinforcements which brought Governor Drucour's garrison to 3,500 soldiers, 2,600 seamen and 1,000 marines. Another warship, the *Magnifique*, reached Louisbourg too early and became caught in the drift-ice. One hundred and twenty of her crew died, twelve from the cold in one night.

The British fleet anchored in Gabarus Bay, six miles south of Louisbourg. Its position was dangerous. With the wind blowing from the east, des Gouttes might slip out of harbour, bear down on the British and inflict considerable damage. But, true to the defensive character of French naval warfare, he remained in port. Several British ships dragged their anchors and were saved with difficulty from being swept ashore.

The French expected the British to land in the bay, where the New Englanders had come ashore. They had erected fortifications along the beach, which sloped upwards, the ground rising in bare shoulders covered by scrub. In the vulnerable area, the 6,000-yard frontage between Cormorant Cove and White Point, elaborate fortifications had been built. Midway in the arc, at Flat Point, rose a watch-tower flanked by abatis, so thickly entwined that it appeared to be a natural grove. On either side lay flat, rock-strewn beaches, rising to 20-foot-high cliffs. Embrasures for cannon and trenches for soldiers had been dug at their summit. The man-made defences were rendered even more formidable by nature; the beaches were pounded by heavy surf. To the most sanguine observers, the defences seemed insurmountable.

Amherst modified his plan. He had intended that his three brigadiers, Wolfe, Lawrence and Whitmore, should land along the beach between Cormorant Cove and White Point, with Wolfe on the left, Lawrence in the centre and Whitmore on the right. 89

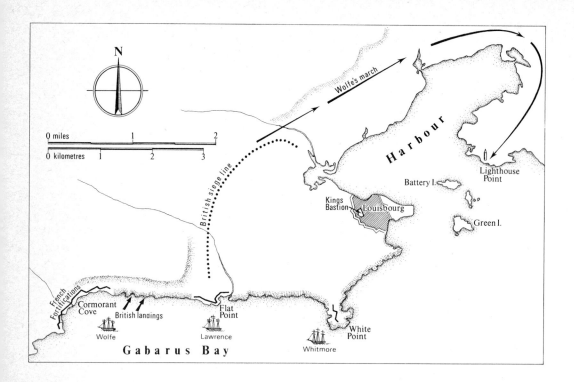

N

0 miles   1   2

0 kilometres   1   2   3

Wolfe's march

British siege line

H a r b o u r

Lighthouse
Point

Battery I.

Kings
Bastion — Louisbourg

Green I.

French Fortifications

Cormorant
Cove
   British landings

Flat
Point

White
Point

Wolfe   Lawrence

Whitmore

G a b a r u s   B a y

The British assault on the French fortress of Louisbourg, on Cape Breton island, the bastion that guarded the St. Lawrence. Following the landing at Gabarus Bay, Wolfe led the army to encircle the garrison, which capitulated on 27 July 1758.

Instead he concentrated his forces against Cormorant Cove. Wolfe would lead the attack and the other two brigadiers would follow him ashore and support him.

On 6 and 7 June the swell, rising breeze and fog prevented a landing. Hoping that it might be better next day, Boscawen gave orders to his captains to have the boats at the transports by midnight. Lights were extinguished and the soldiers were cautioned to prevent accidental discharge of muskets. Wolfe waited on the *Neptune* ready to lead the Grenadiers, Highlanders and Light Infantry, the spearhead of the assault. Just before daybreak Captain Durell returned to report that he had rowed along the shore and that the surf in Cormorant Cove was not too heavy to prevent a landing.

At 4.00 a.m., as it became light, observers on the shore saw three to four hundred boats emerge from behind the sheltering ships and make for Cormorant Cove. The French batteries burst into flame; their fire was returned by the British frigates which manoeuvred dangerously close to land. Very wisely, thought Amherst, the French infantrymen did not throw away a shot until the boats were close inshore. As they came into the cove some boats capsized, throwing the soldiers into the sea. The entire complement

90

of one of the boats, twenty guardsmen and their officer, was drowned. Others were dashed to pieces or stove-in by collision with protruding rocks. The men who kept their feet in the heavy swell tried to scramble up the beach. Wolfe jumped into the water to lead them. 'The difficulty of landing at this place,' stated the author of an anonymous journal, 'was such that they thought the devil himself would not have attempted it.' Realising that it was impossible to achieve a successful landing, Wolfe waved his hat in signal for retreat.

Two young army officers either missed the signal or ignored it. Noticing an undefended stretch of beach, so precipitous and inaccessible that the French had neglected to guard it, they ran their two boats into the 'nest of rocks'. The Light Infantrymen waded ashore. They signalled other boats to follow them into the small creek. Wolfe backed them up at once.

Some time elapsed before these British invaders were noticed. Colonel St Julhein, his vision obscured by the smoke of gunfire, thought that the British boats had withdrawn and were all offshore. By the time he learned of the successful landing it was too late. Several thousand soldiers had come ashore at the creek and had taken cover in a small wood where they dried out and reloaded their muskets. St Julhein's soldiers, exhausted by their week's vigil in the trenches, advanced slowly. They were met by well-directed volleys. They broke and fled, pursued by Wolfe's skirmishers.

Wolfe had made a direct frontal attack on an impregnable position. He agreed that luck had been on his side; 'it may be said we made a rash and ill-advised attempt, and by the greatest good fortune we succeeded'. The two lieutenants, Hopkins and Brown, with Ensign Grant, had saved the day by their brilliant exploit, justifying Wolfe's opinion that 'the greatness of an object should come into consideration as opposed to the implications that lie in its way'. Expressed in modern language, he meant that odds need to be calculated against the possible advantage to be gained.

Attempts to identify the three heroes of the landing have failed. The British army in North America contained two lieutenants named Hopkins, five named Brown and four named Grant. Their enterprise shows that the lower military ranks, unlike some of their seniors, were infused with the spirit of enterprise.

Thanks to these officers, the British had made a successful landing at the small cost of one hundred men. It was still only 8.00 a.m. The French fell back on Louisbourg, leaving the British masters of the coast. The fate of the fortress could only be delayed. 91

Drucour was hindered rather than helped by des Gouttes who clamoured to be allowed to save his fleet by flight. The five warships had the power to impede the siege, Drucour insisted. Between them they mounted twice as many guns as the fort's batteries. 'These ships of war,' stated a British officer, 'did much mischief, retarding the siege greatly, keeping a constant and terrible fire on our works.'

Amherst had his army on shore by 12 June, but a month elapsed before all the heavy guns had been landed. He sent Wolfe, with 1,220 picked men, to march around Louisbourg harbour. He built roads and established gun-emplacements on the western shore, and a seven-gun battery on Lighthouse Point, on the northern shore of the harbour. It commanded the narrow harbour entrance and the two protecting islands, Battery and Rocky. While Wolfe was thus occupied, the army engineers constructed siege lines and gun emplacements to the south of the fortress, work in which they were hampered by the rocky nature of the ground. By 3 July the guns had been advanced to within six hundred yards of the town, into which they threw red-hot shells. One shell fell in the courtyard of the Citadel and another exploded in the crowded hospital, killing a surgeon and dangerously wounding two Sisters of Mercy.

Next morning Drucour sent a letter to Amherst proposing to set apart a place for the sick where they would not be fired upon. In reply Amherst regretted that there was no place within the town where they might be secure. He suggested they should be placed on one of the warships which would be moored in the upper part of the harbour. This meant the loss of a ship to the French, and Drucour refused to agree. This interchange of civilities was marked by the gift from Amherst to Madame Drucour of two pineapples, one of which proved to be rotten, and by Drucour of two bottles of champagne and some butter.

The sluggishness of the siege astonished the French. It exhibited prudence beyond bounds, thought engineer officer Poilly. A French sortie during the night of 9 July failed either to do any damage or hurry the British. On the night of the 15th the frigate *Aréthuse*, with Drucour's permission, slipped out of harbour, carrying to France the Governor's report that the fall of the city could not be longer delayed. Drucour told his government:

The garrison becomes weaker from day to day, the ordinary fate of that of a besieged town, but this is an uncommon and special plight, it has no secure shelter for rest, so here the soldier who is on duty by day passes the night in the open, on the ramparts or in the covered ways. He is overcome with weariness, nevertheless shows great good will which delights, but he cannot hold out.

James Wolfe, the hero of Quebec, who died at the moment of victory. *From the painting by Joseph Highmore*

The taking of Quebec, 13 September, 1759. British reinforcements land as the British and French armies fight on the Plains of Abraham.

The Death of Montcalm.
The artist has erred in
placing the scene on the
field of battle; in fact
Montcalm died of his
wounds later within
Quebec where he was
carried by his soldiers.

Wolfe died on the battle-
field, following a wound
in the thigh. His body
was later taken on
board the *Lowestoft*.
From a tapestry after the
painting by Benjamin West

One-third of the garrison had been killed or wounded. Many of the town's four thousand civilians had died. Their homes had been destroyed, if not by enemy shells, to provide building material for the repair of the fort's dismantled embrasures and emplacements. The store of balls and cartridges began to fail. Iron scraps were used in the mortars, British shot picked up and returned. Madame Drucour toured the battlements; she fired three cannon herself.

On the afternoon of the 21st, a shot struck the *Célèbre* (64 guns), setting alight the powder stored on the poop. The fire raced up the mizzen mast. Sparks blew on to the *Entreprenant* (74). She in turn set fire to the *Capricieux* (64). The *Bienfaisant* (64) escaped by swinging on her cables. Apart from this only the *Prudent* (74) lying to windward escaped. The smoke from the burning battleships hung over the doomed town. An English officer watched the conflagration. He was joined by a chaplain who greatly enjoyed the scene, the source of which he tried to identify:

Oh, Lord, cried an officer, I am afraid our hospital is on fire, what will become of the poor fellows, lame and wounded. The sober divine exclaimed, I am afraid that idle rascal my cook, has set the hut on fire and my piece of beef will be burnt to ashes.

The horror of the conflagration was increased by the loaded guns of the ships, as they became hot, going off, their shells striking other ships and houses in the town. The ships blazed all night, drifting ashore with the tide where they lay with their guns tumbled into their holds. With the loss of these big ships, all further hope of prolonging the siege was ended. Their destruction increased the friction between the navy and army. The irate captain of the Bourgogne regiment had the temerity to claim that he could have saved the ships. The navy clapped him in irons.

On 22 July the King's Bastion, Drucour's home and head-quarters, caught fire. Observing the pall of smoke, the British gunners poured in a storm of balls and shells. Try as they might, the defenders failed to extinguish the flames. Drucour reported:

The few casements were placed in the inner part of the Citadel, in them were shut in the ladies and some of the women of the town, and one was kept for wounded officers. There was every reason to fear that the fire would reach the protections which had been placed in front of these casements, and by the direction of the wind the smoke might stifle the women shut up in them, so that all the women and a great number of little children came out, running to and fro, not knowing where to go in the midst of bombs and balls falling on every side, and among them wounded officers brought out on stretchers, with no safe place to put them.   97

That day the British six-gun battery fired six hundred shells. All night long bombs, some of them charged with combustibles, were hurled into the town. All the French works suffered, and by evening the wooden barracks were on fire and beyond control. The fire was prevented from spreading into the town only by pulling down the neighbouring huts. During the 24th there was no abatement in the bombing. The Queen's Bastion caught fire. Deserters who reached British camps told that the townspeople had entreated the governor to capitulate. The guns at the Citadel were nearly silenced. When they did fire, it seemed to Drucour more like minute guns at a funeral than a defence.

The British brought scaling ladders up to the trenches to be ready for the final assault. The condition of the town was desperate. With the guns at the Citadel finally silenced, the only return fire came from two battered ships in the harbour. Boscawen determined to silence them by a 'cutting out' operation. Captains Balfour and Laforey manned boats from their vessels, the *Etna* and the *Hunter*. On the night of the 25th they entered the harbour, rowing silently towards the French ships. Laforey made for the *Prudent*, aground close to the Batterie de la Grave. The sentinel on the '74' hailed the boat. A voice replied in French that it was from the town and he was coming on board. A French officer called over the side, '*Montez cinq ou six hommes*'. Before he suspected anything, two hundred men were in possession of the deck. The officers were taken captive, guards were placed at the hatchways, twenty British prisoners were released, combustibles placed in the gunroom and ignited. The British sailors scrambled back into their boats and made off. Some shots aroused the town. Drucour went to the Battery and directed the fire of a cannon on the burning ship.

On the *Bienfaisant*, a short conflict followed the boarding. Seven British sailors were killed and nine were wounded before she was carried. The boats towed her to the harbour entrance, opening it to the British fleet. A garrison officer described the disaster:

One is at first surprised to see two great ships letting themselves be taken by little boats, but one's astonishment diminishes when one knows that the officers and the crews kept themselves hidden in the holds of the ships for fear of blows, that they had only a few men on deck to give warning. I do not undertake to say that all the ships did the same, but it is certain that most of them acted in the same way. It is claimed that a naval officer is dishonoured when he hides himself a moment in the hold. On this principle, what should one think of these gentlemen who were so long hidden there? The officers on guard on the *Prudent* and their midshipmen, were quartered in the boatswain's store-room where they were so safe and comfortable that the English were already masters of the ship before they knew anything about it, that there was only one officer got on deck before the English had placed sentinels on the hatchways. The others only came out when they were told to come up and surrender.

Another French officer thought that the conduct of the naval officers merited scorn. They gave no help to the garrison.

Next day Amherst and Boscawen received a letter from Drucour offering to capitulate. The letter was carried by an officer, Loppincot, who on 29 June 1749 had arranged the preliminaries of the return of the fortress to the French. On that occasion he had worn a bright, new uniform, befitting the occasion. Now he came begrimed from the rigours of the siege. Drucour was given one hour to surrender, terms which he thought were humiliating. He laid them before his council. Several officers wished to continue the defence and force the British to storm the last remaining bastion. Drucour sent Loppincot back to the British lines to say that the town would submit only to assault. While Loppincot was on his way, Civil-Commissioner Prevost submitted a memoir pointing out the hardships of the people and the difference between soldiers whose professional duty it was to face horrors, and civilians who were forced to undergo such horrors as awaited them.

Drucour accepted Prevost's views, and officers were despatched to overtake Loppincot. News of the capitulation spread through the town and it was received with joy by the people. It enraged and humiliated the troops. The attitude of the officers verged on sedition. They blamed Drucour for not surrendering two days earlier, when they could have obtained the honours of war, or for surrendering when they could have held out for two more days. The men of the Cambis regiment burnt their colours.

Wolfe admitted that the terms were harsh. Amherst determined to make the most of it: the capture of Louisbourg was Britain's first success in the war.

The garrison laid down their arms on 27 July. At noon the British Grenadier companies marched through the fortress gate, its vaulted roof ringing with the tread of their hobnailed boots.

The garrison had made a valiant defence. Once the British had landed, the result was a foregone conclusion. Wolfe was the moving spirit of the attack. The loss of life was surprisingly small, 195 British killed and 363 wounded, and between 700 and 800 French killed and wounded. The British blew up the remaining fortifications, which were never rebuilt.

News of the fall of Louisbourg reached London on 18 August. It was the first golden ray of Pitt's mounting sun. King George was ecstatically pleased. 'We must keep Cape Breton, take Canada, drive the French out of America, have two armies in Germany', he said: then Britain would be a great nation. His exuberance displeased the Duke of Newcastle, though he agreed it was 'the greatest and most glorious event that ever was', and it must 'do our business'. He believed it would secure peace. Louisbourg could be exchanged for Minorca or Hanover, Pitt would no longer be required and Newcastle could return to his accustomed eminence. Pitt's immediate reaction to the news is not recorded. His wife spoke for him. 'Happy and glorious for my loved England, happy and glorious for my most loved and admired husband.'

Four days later came the news of Abercromby's disaster at Ticonderoga. It disappointed Pitt, who had hoped that the year's campaign would be decisive. 'I own,' he told Grenville, 'this news has sunk my spirits.' Quebec would have to wait another year.

In Europe, Frederick, by skilful manoeuvring, was holding his own, despite his defeat by the Austrians at Hochkirch on 13 October 1758. Ferdinand of Brunswick, who had taken command of the British-subsidized Army of Observation, defeated the French on 23 June at Crefeld, driving the invaders back across the Rhine and ending temporarily the threat to Hanover. In response to Ferdinand's request, Pitt sent ships to the port of Emden. The sailors ousted the French and installed a British garrison. The port's acquisition ensured communications with Ferdinand, whose success caused Pitt to change his mind. Hitherto, in opposition to the King and Newcastle, he had refused to commit British troops to the continental war, preferring to subsidise Britain's allies. In August 1758 he sent twelve squadrons of cavalry, six thousand men including the Emden garrison, to join Ferdinand, to the satisfaction of the Duke of Newcastle who thought that they 'showed our friends that we meant to do something in this war'. Suitably reinforced, Pitt believed, Ferdinand could occupy French troops in Europe and prevent them from being sent to North America.

Pitt's selection of officers proved unfortunate. When they learned that troops were being sent to Germany, his friends, the Duke of Marlborough and Lord George Sackville, demanded to be transferred to that command. In the case of Marlborough, Pitt bowed to necessity for the former held the important office of Master-General of the Ordnance. He was the grandson of the Great Duke, and a man of small ability. He died shortly after his arrival in Germany and Sackville succeeded to the command with dire consequences which Pitt could hardly have foreseen. Both officers had showed up badly in the raid on the French port of St Malo earlier that year. The port was a nest of privateers who preyed upon British shipping. The city merchants clamoured for their destruction. Pitt hoped too to create a diversion which would necessitate the retention of troops in France, to the consequent benefit of Frederick and Ferdinand.

Pitt's choice of a particular naval officer to act as second-in-command of the fleet caused a rift in that service. He selected Richard Howe (one of the three brothers of that name) to serve under Admiral Hawke. Howe was only a junior captain.

Admiral Lord Howe, one of the three brothers who held important commands during the war.

Indignant at this affront to naval dignity, Hawke struck his flag. He was mollified only by Lord Anson's tactful offer to lead the expedition himself. Hawke accepted the inferior status and Howe sailed with the convoy which anchored in Cancale Bay on 4 June. The soldiers marched unopposed into St Malo, destroyed shipping valued at £500,000, and indulged in an orgy of plunder and destruction 'to the reproach of discipline and disgrace of humanity'. On the news of the approach of French troops, the Duke of Marlborough hurriedly re-embarked his men, and the expedition spent the remainder of the month in making ineffective demonstrations against other ports.

During these operations another Howe brother, William, who had chosen a military career, conceived an aversion for Lord George Sackville, due it is thought to that officer's reluctance to fight. Whatever was the cause of the dispute, Howe carried his hostility to the next war in which he served for two years as Commander-in-Chief of the British army in America under the authority of the Secretary of State for the Colonies, Lord George Germain, the name Sackville had adopted. The strained relations of these two men contributed to the British defeat at Saratoga, the turning point of that war.

On the return to England of Marlborough's force, it was re-organised and entrusted to the command of the aged General Thomas Bligh. With the naval squadron now led by Richard Howe, the future Admiral, Bligh captured Cherbourg, dismantled its forts and burned shipping. But as at St Malo, the approach of French troops precipitated retreat. Bligh failed to re-embark his troops before they were attacked, losing more than a thousand men.

Pitt boasted to Frederick that by these raids and excursions he had occupied thirty thousand French troops who might otherwise have been sent to Germany.

Another expedition was more directly rewarding to Britain. Early in 1758 the city merchant, Thomas Cumming, drew Pitt's attention to the possibility of capturing the French trading stations in West Africa. This suggestion, offering the opportunity of profit, appealed to Pitt. He despatched Captain Henry Marsh with two ships of the line and four smaller vessels, carrying two hundred marines commanded by Major Mason. The squadron reached the mouth of the Senegal river in April, to find that its estuary was guarded by a fort built on an island ten miles above the sand-bar against which waves dashed with great violence. Lacking a local pilot, Marsh required ten days to sail his ships, one of sixty-four guns and another of fifty, up river. Mason successfully landed his

Opposite The *Warspite* cruising off Goree, the French West African trading post which fell to the British.

marines and artillery. This demonstration of military might caused the French garrison to surrender. The British captured rich booty, ivory, gold dust, trade goods and slaves. Many civilians rejected the offer of repatriation to France, preferring to stay with their native wives whom one Frenchman described as 'perfect beauties'.

Marsh sailed on to the island of Goree, the principal French trading station. Finding it too strong to conquer, he returned to England. In December 1758 Pitt sent a more powerful fleet commanded by Commodore Augustus Keppel. His massed broadsides demolished the fort and completed the ruin of the French trade, with consequent benefit to the victors who were thus provided with an additional source of wealth.

Pitt had even more ambitious plans to deprive the French of their colonial possessions by exploiting Britain's strength and France's weakness at sea. The French Caribbean islands of Martinique and Guadeloupe exported annually a million pounds' worth of commodities, including sugar, their chief crop. This flourishing trade was derived from the labour of a hundred and fifty thousand negro slaves and the commercial activities of forty thousand white planters. An intercepted letter written by a resident of Martinique suggested that the island was ripe for conquest.

This poor Country, which you once knew in a flourishing state, has been afflicted within three years by two dreadful Hurricans, which have forever ruined one third of the Inhabitants; by a War, more dreadful than can be imagined; and to compleat our misery, by a Drought, which continued from the beginning of this year, ruins all our Plantations and affords a very melancholy Prospect for the ensuing Year. May God have Mercy upon us, and at least grant us a Peace, no matter on what Condition.

The acquisition of these strategic islands would change the balance of power in the Caribbean. Due to the prevailing easterly wind the French held the advantage. Fleets coming from Europe, once they had passed the Leeward Islands, could not return the same way. Blown westwards, they were forced to round San Domingo or Cuba. The British island of Jamaica, with its excellent harbour at Kingston, was too far west to control the inward sailing passage. Barbados, isolated on the Leeward fringe, had no harbour. The only British Leeward base was at English Harbor, Antigua. As well as holding Martinique and Guadeloupe in the east, the French possessed a westward base at Cap François on the northern coast of San Domingo. Cuba and Puerto Rico were owned by Spain.

Martinique was also an important privateering base. It could be

Opposite Commodore Augustus Keppel, who, commanded the fleet which finally reduced the French West African trading post at Goree.

The Caribbean Sea and West Indies 1754–1763, showing British, French and Spanish provinces at the start of the war. The British took Martinique, Guadeloupe, St Lucia and Cuba only to return them at the conclusion of peace.

exchanged, calculated Pitt, for Minorca at the conclusion of peace. Meanwhile its harbours could be denied to the vessels which had been preying upon British and American shipping. Lord Anson opposed Pitt's plan to send a fleet to the West Indies, as he feared that his best ships would be difficult to recall should a sudden emergency require their presence in home waters. Ignoring the First Lord's objections Pitt commandeered eight ships of the line, including the 90-gun vessel the *St George*. For the army command he was forced to accept the King's choice of Major-General Thomas Hopson, an old and worn-out officer, giving him six thousand soldiers. On the fleet's arrival at Barbados, it fell under the command of Commodore Moore who added four ships of the line from his West Indian squadron. The combined force arrived off Martinique on 13 January.

The tiny island burst into world fame in 1902 when the volcano Pelée exploded, destroying within two minutes the town of St Pierre and suffocating all but two of its thirty thousand inhabitants. The island's chief port in 1758, Fort Royal, lay twenty miles distant from the then dormant volcano. Less strongly fortified than the island's capital, it offered better opportunity for attack.

106

The navy bombarded the fort's batteries, while the army established a beach-head some distance from the town. The soldiers held their ground in the face of a French counter-attack, but the heavy surf prevented the landing of guns. Hopson re-embarked his troops, unaware that the French governor was preparing to blow up his fortifications and depart. The fleet returned to St Pierre where Captain Jekyl navigated his 50-gun ship, the *Rippon*, close to the shore to test the defences, coming under the fire of the powerful French batteries. In vain he replied with his broadsides and stern-chase guns. An unusual leeward wind held the ship and the crew were forced to take to the boats to warp her off-shore. Moore and Hopson agreed that Martinique was too strong to capture.

They sailed for another thirty miles to Guadeloupe. The island, the largest of the Windward Group, is really two islands, Basse-Terre and Grande-Terre, forming fifty square miles of land divided by a narrow strait. Fort Royal, the principal town on Basse-Terre, overlooked an open roadstead, its great depth of water enabling the fleet to manoeuvre close inshore. The broad-sides of eight ships of the line silenced the fort's guns. Stray shots set fire to the houses in the town, and by midnight, as Moore told Pitt, it presented a 'dreadful scene of conflagration'. The garrison abandoned the town and took up an impregnable position four miles away on the mountain pass known locally as 'the ass's back', where it was believed twenty men could defy ten thousand. The British troops occupied the town.

While Hopson considered his next move, Moore detached ships which hammered the privateering base at Pointe-à-Pitre on Grande-Terre, smashing the port's installations and reducing the town to ashes. Unaccustomed to the climate, the troops became decimated by fever and Hopson himself died. The new commander, John Barrington, a favourite of Pitt's, and his own original choice, secured volunteers from the British West Indian islands. He landed his troops midway between Guadeloupe and Martinique, while Moore took the fleet to Dominica, to watch for the French fleet which had been sighted. This fleet, commanded by Maxim Bompar, had slipped out of Brest.

Advancing from town to town, Barrington brought about the island's capitulation. Too late, Bompar, who had eluded Moore, landed six hundred regulars and the 'buccaneers' he had recruited from Martinique. Fearing attack by Moore's more powerful fleet, Bompar re-embarked his men and sailed away.

The capitulation of Guadeloupe reduced the chief French

Overleaf The British capture Martinique, the chief French naval base in the Caribbean, an amphibious operation led by Admiral Rodney.

107

possessions in the Caribbean to the islands of Martinique and San Domingo (the Spanish Hispaniola and the modern Haiti). Within the year Guadeloupe was sending to Britain £425,000 worth of sugar. Pitt was not satisfied. He sent an even more powerful expedition in 1761 which captured Martinique. The army was commanded by Major-General Robert Monckton who, as we shall learn, had distinguished himself in North America. The powerful fleet of eighteen ships of the line and fourteen frigates was led by Rear-Admiral Rodney who thus familiarised himself with the waters, between the islands of St Lucia and Martinique, where twenty-one years later he won the great victory of 'the Saints' over Admiral de Grasse.

In 1761 the citizens of Martinique took the oath of submission to the British Crown, Rodney remarking 'they seem quite satisfied with their new condition, for they are indulged in everything they desire and, I believe, were never so happy before', possibly the first recorded instance of British belief that, by conquering a foreign people, they were conferring upon them the ineffable benefits of British democracy.

Following the fall of Martinique, the French islands of St Lucia, Grenada and St Vincent, and their trade, came into British possession. Pitt had made a clean sweep of French possessions in the Caribbean, strangling her economic life. As the war progressed, British trade flourished, French trade declined. To fight the war in 1759, Parliament granted Pitt £20 million. France, with her far greater population, could raise only £14 million.

Yet Newcastle clamoured for peace, pleading mounting expense and financial stringency. The only way to have peace is to prepare for war, Pitt told his timid colleague. The balance was swinging in Britain's favour, and the Duke admitted his own inadequacy. 'If Mr Pitt went now I should think myself a traitor to the King if I pretended to undertake the carrying on of his affairs.' Strong as was Pitt's position, the Duc de Choiseul, the new French minister, detected his weakness. 'He knows he will have to quit office the moment his master has no further need of him, which will be the moment peace is signed.'

The Duc de Choiseul gained power in France too late to pose a real threat to Pitt or to remedy the defects of despotic rule. 'Peace is the only remedy, that is your task,' his predecessor, the Abbé Bernis, told him. Pitt recognised the capabilities of his new rival. 'Since the days of Cardinal Richelieu, France has had no minister as great as Choiseul.' Choiseul determined to fight until France's last enemies were destroyed. To gain that end he told France's

ambassador in Madrid to urge the Spanish King to 'make common cause with us'. Only the combination of their two navies could overcome British superiority at sea.

The Duc de Choiseul, France's chief minister who outwitted Lord Bute in the peace negotiations.

Chapter 7

Quebec

*the words are missing —

But since ignoble age* must come,
disease & death's inexorable doom,
That life which others pay let us bestow
And give to fame what we to nature owe:

The moment he heard of the fall of Louisbourg, Pitt began to plan the attack on Quebec, on which three armies would converge simultaneously. He was confident that his young generals could conquer Canada in 1759. Amherst, who had been given the overall command in North America, would push up the north–south waterway from New York to Canada, via the Hudson river, Lakes George and Champlain and the Richelieu river to Montreal. Another expedition would sweep westwards and circle round through Lakes Erie and Ontario. The main force would ascend the St Lawrence river to Quebec, which would be a stupendous undertaking. For a fleet to carry an army hundreds of miles up a river through hostile territory to assault a fortress defended by regular troops was without precedent. The hazards of navigating the St Lawrence were legendary. Should the main force overcome these difficulties, the other two might not. Pitt's strategy of concentration of maximum force could fail. Any one of the three expeditions might be delayed. No single expedition was sufficiently powerful to succeed on its own, unless it surprised the French or took terrible risks.

Pitt gambled on French weakness, on his knowledge that however ill the war had gone for Britain, the French had suffered more. He believed that the French Empire in North America was breaking up. One crushing blow was required to effect its demise.

Pitt guessed correctly. 'Canada is surrounded on every side,' Montcalm believed. Governor de Vaudreuil expected 'attack from every side'. Bigot, the Intendent or Civil Commissioner, declared 'we are hemmed in on every side'. The three officers agreed that there was only one solution to their troubles: 'Peace or Canada is lost'.

The French Canadians were on their knees. Four years of blockade had taken heavy toll. Weakened by famine, decimated by disease, lacking replacements to make good the losses of war, the Canadian army stood at half strength. The home government had abandoned the colony to its fate. Canada's 'immense open spaces' were not worth the cost. The wealth of princes, it was thought, derived from the number of their subjects. The Caribbean sugar islands were more valuable than Canada's snowy wastes.

To Canada's pleas for help, the French government replied that it had no ships or reinforcements to send, that the Canadians must redouble their efforts, call up all men fit to bear arms, their youths and old men, and fight to the last, in order to enable France to secure better terms at the peace. 'The memory of what you did

Opposite James Wolfe; the drawing made by the Duchess of Devonshire before Wolfe's departure for North America. This portrait was found with these lines of verses in Wolfe's pocket after his death at Quebec.

113

last year leads his Majesty to hope once again you will find means to foil their [British] plans,' the government instructed Montcalm. Following his defeat of Abercromby at Ticonderoga, Montcalm had become the darling of the French court. With only four thousand Frenchmen he had defeated twenty thousand British soldiers. De Vaudreuil blamed Montcalm for his failure to pursue and destroy the demoralised British army.

De Vaudreuil and Montcalm disagreed how best to defend Canada. Montcalm expected the British to invade with over-whelming forces, and advocated a purely defensive strategy, believing that Quebec was impregnable. His wish to abandon the frontier posts was opposed by de Vaudreuil, who wanted to defend the frontier fort by fort. He believed that the conquest of the Province would be a 'work of great difficulty, not to say impos-sibility'. Montcalm laughed to scorn de Vaudreuil's scheme, calling it 'the Council of quacks'. De Vaudreuil was equally caustic about Montcalm's plan. 'Monsieur de Montcalm,' he told the Minister of Marine, 'and the land troops seek only to preserve their reputations and would like to return to France without having suffered a single defeat.'

The two generals sent emissaries to Paris to plead their cause. Montcalm chose the better advocate, his aide Colonel Bougain-ville, the one-time diplomat turned soldier.

On 20 December, the French Council of Ministers agreed that such divergent views were dangerous. They recommended to the King that Montcalm should be recalled and replaced by his second-in-command, the Chevalier Lévis. Then Bougainville appeared. Meeting again on 28 December, the Ministers reversed themselves. 'Monsieur de Montcalm is necessary in the present conjuncture,' they advised the King. The Minister of War, the veteran Marshal Belle-Isle, supported Montcalm. He persuaded Louis XV to promote him to Lieutenant-General, a rank above that held by de Vaudreuil. The Governor was ordered to consult with Montcalm on all operations and employ Montcalm's defensive strategy, to allow the British to advance into the heart of New France. De Vaudreuil was instructed to maintain a foothold in North America.

De Vaudreuil based his confidence on the belief that the British would not dare ascend the St Lawrence. It was rudely shaken when Bougainville brought news that the British were preparing a great naval and military armament. The secret had been disclosed in Pitt's letter to Amherst. It had been intercepted and copied by a French spy.

Colonel Bougainville who commanded one of the French armies at Quebec and who, in later life, became an explorer of the Pacific.

On 29 December, Pitt sent detailed instructions to Amherst, the overall commander of the three-pronged invasion in Canada. Pitt incorporated his orders in a four-thousand-word letter. His Majesty, he said, had 'Nothing so much at heart as to improve the great and important advantages gained in the last campaign, as well as to repair the Disappointment at Ticonderoga, and, by the most vigorous and decisive Efforts, to establish, by the Blessings of God on his Arms, His Majesty's just and indubitable Rights, and to avert all future Dangers to His Majesty's subjects in North America.' Having satisfied protocol, Pitt got down to business.

Wolfe would command 12,500 men in the operation against Quebec, proceeding from Louisbourg up the St Lawrence river. He would take the rank of Major-General for that expedition only. Amherst was enjoined to cause certain named regiments to assemble on Cape Breton island by 20 April, so that they could proceed up river by 7 May, and to provide all proper provisions (and particularly fresh provisions as far as possible), 'with the utmost Diligence', put the battering train in the most perfect repair, and direct engineers and artillery to take part. Twenty thousand tons of transport vessels would be sent from England to New York, to convey troops and equipment. Nonetheless, Amherst himself should provide six thousand tons of transports to guard against the non-arrival or lateness of vessels from England. So that he should not fail to provide such transports, Amherst was instructed to place an embargo on the use of these vessels. This embargo would endure until such time as transports actually sailed for their destination. But Amherst was not to mention the circumstances, the reasons for the embargo, for fear that the requisitioned transports 'may not be altogether so nearly ready at the same time as is to be wished'.

Pitt also spelled out other services which Amherst should not omit to provide; to supply, with the utmost diligence, eighty carpenters, a troop of Rangers, bateaux-men, not less than forty schooners and sloops and seventy whale-boats. He should also provide a garrison of Provincial troops for Louisbourg during the absence of the King's forces.

Amherst himself would lead the 'irruption' into Canada by way of Ticonderoga, Crown Point and Lake Champlain in order to attack Montreal and Quebec. It was also the King's pleasure that he give attention to the operation on Lake Ontario, to capture Fort Niagara, and to 'establish uninterrupted Dominion of that lake'. He was instructed at the same time to urge and quicken the Colonists to expedite the mobilisation of their levies, their supplies to be provided by the King. Nor did Pitt forget the 'Health of the Men'. When possible they were to be supplied with fresh meat (both beef and pork), and provided with arms and tents.

Pitt's letter to Wolfe, informing him of his promotion to command the chief expedition against Quebec and ordering him to remain in North America, reached Nova Scotia after Wolfe had sailed for England. His presence in London displeased Pitt, until the confusion was explained. Wolfe had returned to repair his health, as a result of his understanding with Lord Ligonier, the Captain-General of the Forces. Wolfe suffered from tuberculosis and kidney deficiency, derived it is thought from the hardships of a life in the army which he had joined at the age of fifteen. He had served at Fontenoy and at Culloden, and had distinguished himself with Mordaunt at Rochefort. He was barely thirty-two years of age. He had no objection, he told Pitt, to serving in America and particularly in the St Lawrence. He asked only for time to repair the injury to his constitution, when Mr Pitt could 'dispose of my slight carcase as he pleases'. He would rather die than decline the service offered. Privately he complained, 'It is my fortune to be cursed with American service'.

Wolfe, like many serving officers, hankered after service in Europe with Prince Ferdinand or King Frederick. His ambition was to make a name as a cavalry commander. He had another desire, to marry the heiress niece of Sir John Lowther, an important figure in British politics, the future Earl of Lonsdale. Wolfe had courted Katherine Lowther for two years. As an impecunious Colonel his suit had not prospered, but as a Major-General, the hero of the hour was welcomed as a prospective relative.

Pitt had hoped to procure permanent rather than local promotion for Wolfe. He failed to overcome the objections raised by the Duke of Newcastle, who saw in the appointment of a young man with no family connections a challenge to his system of private patronage. He carried his fears about Wolfe to the King, telling him 'this man is mad.' 'Mad, is he?' replied George, 'then I hope he will bite some of my other Generals.'

Pitt gave Wolfe three young brigadiers. Only one, George Townsend, was older than Wolfe. Townsend was Newcastle's nephew and protégé. Townsend resented the promotion of an even younger officer and a man of lower family station over his head. The other two brigadiers were both sons of peers, Robert Monckton, Viscount Galway's son, and Lord Elibank's son, James Murray. They had both served in North America and at the Siege of Louisbourg. Pitt overcame the King's hostility to the appointment as Quarter-Master-General of Lieutenant-Colonel Guy Carleton, who had dared to speak slightingly of George II's Hanoverian troops. Isaac Barré became Adjutant-General and Patrick Mc-Kellar retained the office of Chief Engineer which he had held in the Louisbourg expedition. In the selection of naval commander Pitt had a free hand. Vice-Admiral Sir Charles Saunders had sailed round the world with Lord Anson, and had recently commanded the Mediterranean squadron. Wolfe and Saunders struck up an immediate friendship.

Wolfe sailed in the *Neptune* on 14 February with Saunders and fourteen warships and sixty lesser craft. Louisbourg harbour, their destination, was still blocked by ice, and the fleet sailed on to Halifax, arriving there on 30 April. Vice-Admiral Philip Durell was there. Due to the ice-floes, the result of an unprecedentedly severe winter, he had been unable to carry out Pitt's order to cruise in the estuary of the St Lawrence in order to intercept French ships.

By his dilatory behaviour, Durell had jeopardised the expedi-

Admiral Sir Charles Saunders, the unsung hero who made possible Wolfe's victory at Quebec.

tion's success. It was imperative that relief should not reach Quebec. Durell sailed on 5 May. He was too late. Five French frigates, convoying twenty-three store ships, reached Quebec on 5 June. They carried three hundred recruits, provisions, and, worst of all, Bougainville and the copy of Pitt's intercepted letter. Wolfe's and Saunders' attack on Quebec would no longer be a surprise. Had they reached Quebec unannounced they might have taken the city almost without striking a blow, but the warning gave Montcalm time to prepare his defences.

Thirteen days were required at Halifax to embark the troops, the majority of whom came from New York. Their number fell short of the twelve thousand soldiers promised by Pitt. Wolfe had at his command less than nine thousand men, Saunders more than thirty thousand seamen.

The armada, 29 ships of the line, 13 frigates and 119 transports and other vessels, 'the finest squadron that had ever appeared in North America', entered the Gulf of St Lawrence on 15 June. Durell forged ahead, sailing close to the Ile-aux-Coudres, the French pilot station, sixty-five miles from Quebec. When the ships hoisted French flags, the pilots paddled out in their canoes and were taken aboard. Durell also acquired charts from three captured provision ships.

The decoyed pilots and the stolen charts may not have been necessary. The British Major Knox thought that French accounts of the hazards of the navigation of the St Lawrence were a 'bug-bear'. The Master of the transport *Goodwill* refused to allow the French pilot to navigate his ship through the notorious Traverse, the rock-strewn tortuous passage between the Ile-d'Orléans and the shore. When the pilot expostulated, old Killick told him 'Aye, aye, but I'll convince you that an Englishman shall go where no Frenchman dares to show his nose'. Killick put boats over the side, directing his men to row ahead, sounding as they went. He stood at the prow of his vessel, calling to his men, 'Aye, aye, my dears, chalk it down a damned dangerous navigation. If you don't make a splutter about it you will get no credit in England.' Killick declared there were a thousand more dangerous places in the Thames. He navigated the channel without touching a rock.

The main fleet followed Durell, joining his squadron on the southern shore of the Ile-d'Orléans on 25 June. Not a single ship had suffered damage. The Canadians thought it an unbelievable feat. Never before had a fleet navigated the dreaded St Lawrence without suffering a single mishap. That night signal fires flared along the shore, warning the garrison of Quebec that Wolfe was within five miles of his objective.

Wolfe knew that his expedition was one of three designed to converge on Quebec.

Brigadier John Prideaux brought two thousand regulars to Oswego on Lake Erie, and was joined there on 27 June by Sir William Johnson. He had persuaded a thousand Indians from the tribes of the Six Nations to accompany the expedition to capture Fort Niagara. This protected the falls between Lakes Erie and Ontario and was the bulwark of Montreal, across the latter lake and down the St Lawrence. Niagara was the centre of the French fur trade, the basis of Canada's economic wealth. It provided also 119 the advance post from which an attempt to recapture Fort Duquesne, or Fort Pitt as it was now named, could be launched.

The French commander at Niagara, the Chevalier Pouchot, was unaware of the presence of the British army at Oswego. His Indian scouts had failed to detect it and the corvette *Iroquois*, sent to reconnoitre returned to report no sign of the British on the lake. Pouchot commanded 150 regular soldiers and 315 colonists. The old fort had been considerably strengthened by de Vaudreuil who based his defensive strategy on its prolonged resistance.

Prideaux and Johnson landed their men a mile and a half from the fort and by 14 June had run entrenchments to within two hundred and fifty yards. Six days later they had progressed to within eighty yards and were bombarding the fort. Prideaux was killed by the accidental explosion of a British mortar and Johnson succeeded to the command. He successfully ambushed the relief force, marching from the Great Carrying Place and taking seventeen French officers prisoner. His message to Pouchot informing him of their capture induced the fort's commander to surrender. Brigadier Thomas Gage, who came to succeed Prideaux, took his force across Lake Ontario to the headwaters of the St Lawrence within sixty miles of Montreal, but failed to progress further. His presence there induced Montcalm on 10 August to despatch eight hundred men to guard the western approach to Montreal, thus denuding the garrison of Quebec.

Amherst led the other expedition, the attempt to capture Montreal from the south, via the natural waterway, up Lake George and across Lake Champlain. It was guarded by three strongpoints, Forts Ticonderoga and Crown Point, and the Ile-aux-Noix on the Richelieu river. Having overcome the two forts, Amherst would need to build a navy to destroy the French ships cruising on Lake Champlain.

The considerable British force, composed of seven regiments and Colonial levies, eleven thousand soldiers, reached the head of Lake George on 21 July. Amherst disembarked his troops and marched to surround Fort Ticonderoga, no longer the unknown quantity of the previous year. During the winter it had been reconnoitred by the American Ranger Robert Rogers, who brought with him Engineer-Lieutenant Brehm. Together they prowled on snow-shoes around the fort's perimeter, observing the seven and a half foot high log-wall and noting that the ground had been cleared in front, leaving no cover for an attacking force. While Brehm inspected the fort in bright moonlight from the overlooking sugar loaf hill, Rogers and his men captured several Frenchmen

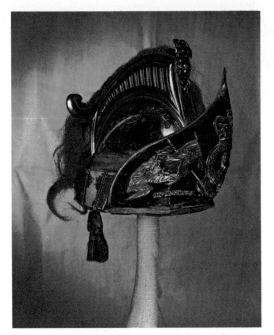

Above left A farrier of the 7th Dragoon Guards.

Above A trooper of the 6th Inniskilling Dragoons at the time of the Seven Years War.

Left The Emsdorf Helmet. The use of the word 'Emsdorf' by the newly-raised 15th Light Dragoons was the first, and for thirty years the only, battle honour in the British Army.

The Battle of Minden,
1759, at which the
British infantry
distinguished themselves,
and the cavalry, due to

Lord George Sackville's
'hesitation', failed to
clinch the victory which
the Allied Army,
commanded by Prince

Ferdinand of Brunswick,
had won over the
French Army.

who provided information about the fort's newly-built defences.

The City of Quebec with the British ships in the foreground.

The fort's commander, Bourlamaque, had at his command four thousand soldiers, about the same number as Montcalm had had in 1758. He had been ordered by Montcalm to abandon and destroy the fort directly the British appeared in strength. Leaving four hundred men to delay the enemy and fire the fuses, the garrison took to their boats, an operation they could not conceal from Amherst, who nonetheless failed to move his artillery to the point from where he could have successfully shelled the departing Frenchmen. The fort, or rather its dismantled bastions, fell into British hands on 26 July. Leaving men to rebuild its defences, Amherst took his army to Crown Point to find that the retreating Frenchmen had also destroyed that fort. He could move no further, due to the presence on the lake of four armed ships. He set his boatmen to build a fleet to command the lake, a task which was not accomplished until 11 October, by which time the onset of winter had ended campaigning. One incident deserves mention: in September Major Robert Rogers, leading two hundred Rangers, waded and splashed through the wilderness to destroy the village of the St Francis Indians, who had made many bloody forays against the American settlers. The story has been told by Kenneth Roberts in his novel *North West Frontier*.

Other than by drawing away some of Quebec's defenders, neither expedition had helped Wolfe. He was on his own.

123

Wolfe scanned Quebec's defences through his telescope.

Three miles away, Quebec city rose on the three hundred foot high bluff of a precipitous promontory, its walls bristling with 106 cannon, its houses descending to the shore of the thirteen hundred yards wide basin of the upper St Lawrence. A floating battery, mounting twelve guns, protected the landing place. To the city's right, the northern shoreline rose steeply until, opposite the Ile-d'Orléans, it was intersected by the deep gorge of the Montmorency river. This shore was protected by a line of redoubts, embrasures and batteries, extending for eight miles. Behind, at Beauport, lay the French camp containing the bulk of Quebec's defenders. The ground between the camp and Quebec was divided by yet another deep and impassable gorge formed by the St Charles river. A bridge of boats across its estuary connected the camp to the city. To the west of Quebec steep cliffs, seven to eight miles in extent, rose above the river. Their heights, Wolfe was told, were named the Plains of Abraham.

Quebec was a natural fortress, apparently unassailable from either flank and impregnable from the front; and Montcalm commanded five thousand regular troops and twelve thousand militiamen, several thousand more men than Wolfe had.

What did Wolfe intend? Having reached his objective, he was uncertain what to do, how to overcome Montcalm's defences. According to school history books, Wolfe, like Julius Caesar on a previous occasion, came, saw and conquered. In fact, Quebec's natural defences placed Wolfe in a dilemma beyond his capacity for decision. Direct assault on the city invited disaster. Slow bombardment offered no solution, for it would not harm Montcalm's army and would take far too long. Quebec must be taken, or the attempt abandoned for another year, before the onset of winter. As long as Montcalm held the northern shore and controlled the river above Quebec, he could not be starved into surrender.

Wolfe had hoped to catch Montcalm unawares, land his troops on the shore to the east of Quebec, march his troops round the base of the triangle formed by the promontory on which the city stood, and invest Quebec on three sides. He reckoned, 'we shall have a smart action at the passage of the river St Charles', unless 'we can steal a detachment up the river St Lawrence', landing there, three, four, five or more miles above the town. From his vantage point on the Ile-d'Orléans, Wolfe saw that Montcalm had frustrated his plan. The defences lining the shore to the east of the city barred access from that direction. Curiously, in the light of later events, Wolfe thought no more of landing above Quebec. Montcalm had blocked Wolfe: on de Vaudreuil's advice he had concentrated his army to the east of the city. He had wanted to place it to the west, on the Plains of Abraham.

The siege of Quebec became a battle of wits between the cautious Frenchman and the impulsive Englishman. One mistake,

The British boats carrying the invasion force which scaled the cliffs above Quebec city.

the taking of one uncalculated risk, could end the siege. Between the two generals lay one difference – Montcalm did not need to take risks, Wolfe had to.

Wolfe has been described as the great master of amphibious operations, a soldier of originality of mind, with scientific mastery of his profession. He has also been described as a man of violent character, quick of temper, emotional and vehement. That professional cynic Horace Walpole pronounced him vainglorious, saying that 'the world could not expect more of him than he thought himself capable of performing'. It is hard to assess Wolfe's intentions. He did not live to write a full report of his operations. We know what he achieved, rather than why he did it. There are two opinions, of which one asserts that when all seemed lost Wolfe rose to the occasion and won victory by a master-stroke. The other claims that he took an appalling risk. It succeeded only because Montcalm committed an appalling blunder. Whatever is the correct interpretation, Wolfe, in July 1759, was bewildered.

Two days after it had anchored in the channel between the Ile-d'Orléans and the southern shore of the St Lawrence, the fleet was struck by a hurricane, so vehement that Montcalm thought that a French fleet, placed in similar circumstances, would have perished. Though some British ships dragged their anchors, none were harmed. A number of whale-boats and cutters were dashed on the rocks and were lost. Next day, 28 June, the French launched their fireships and rafts. They caught fire prematurely

126

and the British sailors had no difficulty in grappling the hulks and beaching them harmlessly. To overcome such perils, Admiral Saunders considered it necessary to move the fleet into the wide basin in front of Quebec. This necessitated the landing of troops and the establishment of batteries on the Ile-d'Orléans and at Pointe Lévis, the promontory on the southern shore commanding the basin.

Brigadier Townsend landed his men on the island and established batteries on its western tip, facing Quebec. Monckton marched his four brigades along the southern shore and, driving off its one thousand defenders, occupied Pointe Lévis. Montcalm had wished to fortify that position but had been overruled by de Vaudreuil, who insisted that Quebec could not be bombarded from that point. Realising the threat posed to the city, Montcalm sent floating batteries in an attempt to dislodge the invaders. The attackers were driven off by the broadsides of a frigate sent by Saunders. During the next ten weeks, the Pointe Lévis batteries pulverised Quebec, destroying its houses and silencing its guns.

Colonel Dumas, Braddock's conqueror, led a counter-attack on to the Ile-d'Orléans. His troops landed at night, divided into two parties, mistook each other for the enemy, fired on their own men and fled in panic. The French made another attempt to destroy the British fleet, anchored now in the basin, by fireships. Once again the sailors grappled the hulks and towed them ashore, where they burnt out harmlessly.

The British disembarked on the southern shore of the St Lawrence. Attempts by the Canadian militia and their Indians, whom Montcalm had posted there, to harass the soldiers led to the terrorisation of the Canadian families living and farming on that side of the river. British foraging parties were ambushed and, according to Sergeant John Johnson, 'butchered in the most cruel and barbarous manner; being first killed and scalped, and then ripped open and their hearts taken out and themselves left on the spot where this horrid barbarity was committed'.

The militia forced the farmers to withhold supplies from the British and to snipe at stray looters. Wolfe forbade reprisals against 'the industrious peasant, the sacred orders of religion, or defenceless women and children'. Offenders, he decreed, would be punished by death. The inhabitants were warned not to take up arms as they would subject themselves to the destruction of their homes and harvests by the exasperated soldiery. Wolfe later reversed his conciliatory policy, burning crops and villages and terrorising the *habitants*, as the French peasants were called.

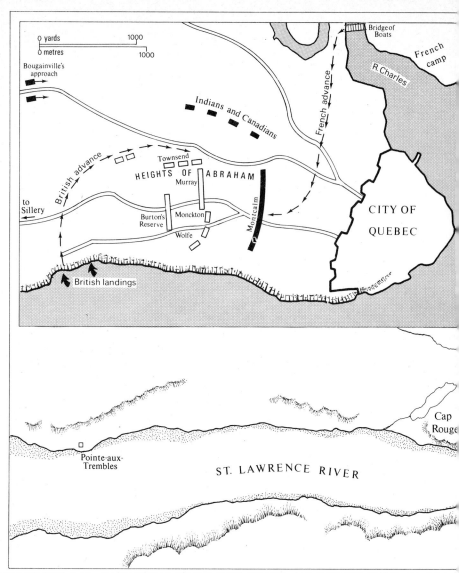

The siege of Quebec, 1759. Following his failure to storm the French lines east of the city. Wolfe achieved victory by carrying his soldiers above Quebec. On the night of September 12/13, the army scaled the cliffs at the Foulon Pass and marched on to the Plains of Abraham, taking the French by surprise.

Wolfe does not seem to have known what to do next. He hoped to bring Montcalm to battle; his motley army would be no match for the disciplined British regulars. But how could he lure Montcalm out of his impregnable defences? Wolfe hoped to do that by carrying his army across the river and placing it on Montcalm's flank. His survey of the shore ruled out direct frontal attack on the camp at Beauport. One of the navy's boats was seized by Indians who paddled out in their canoes, but the frigate *Porcupine*, commanded by the future Admiral Jervis who gained a famous victory over the Spanish fleet at St Vincent in 1797, managed to sail close

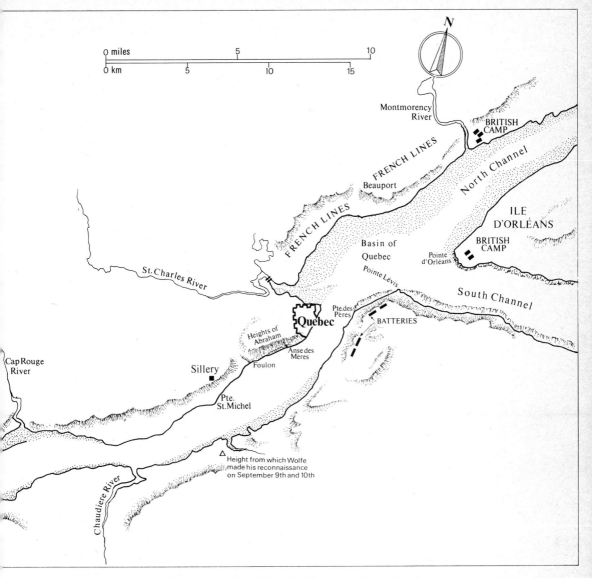

under the camp, a feat never dared by the French pilots. To deceive
Montcalm, Wolfe sent Monckton marching his troops in full view
of Quebec westwards along the southern shore. Several frigates
sailed across the basin to engage the French batteries between the
St Charles and Montmorency rivers. Next day, 9 July, Wolfe
ordered Townsend's and Murray's brigades across the St Lawrence.

Wolfe led the assault himself, to the dismay of Brigadier
Townsend who resented his interference. Townsend reacted by
meticulous personal attention to every detail of the landing,
slowing the advance to the fury of Wolfe. The French hardly op- 129

posed the landing east of the Montmorency gorge, and their counter-attack was easily repulsed. The British set up camp and entrenched themselves, an undertaking which precipitated yet another clash between Wolfe and Townsend. The brigadier complained that his superior was always finding fault, other officers took offence at Wolfe's high-handed methods. This powerful coterie threatened Wolfe, as he wrote, with a parliamentary enquiry into his conduct.

Wolfe's invasion of the northern shore failed in its primary object, to bring Montcalm to battle. Montcalm remained within his defences, secure behind the impassable Montmorency gorge. Lévis urged him to dislodge Wolfe. Montcalm realised that to drive the British off would lead to more serious trouble elsewhere; 'While they are there they cannot hurt us, let them amuse themselves'. The opposing generals exchanged the customary boasts and braggadocio. During the operation of a flag of truce for the exchange of prisoners, Montcalm told Wolfe, 'We do not doubt that you will demolish the town, yet we are determined that your army shall never set foot within its walls'. Wolfe replied that he would be master of Quebec, even if he stayed until the end of November.

The French Indians harassed the British outposts. Sergeant Johnson, who had crossed the river with the grenadiers, recorded their activities:

As soon as the victim is within their aim, they fire and very often kill him dead on the spot; for they very seldom miss their aim, being excellent marksmen. However that may be, they immediately spring up to him and with their butt strike at his head and endeavour to beat out his brains. If upon their advance towards him they discover any signs of resistance, they again take shelter as near the victim as possible, and then taking a cool and deliberate aim they throw their tomahawk, an instrument made in the shape of our camp hatchets, the head not quite so large, with a sharp turn on the back of the head, resembling a hawk's bill, and a longer handle, but not so thick as our camp hatchet's; which they throw with great certainty for a considerable distance and seldom miss.

No sooner have they delivered the tomahawk out of their hands but they spring up to him with their scalping knife, which is made in every respect like our kitchen carving knives, and generally at the first approach rip him open and sometimes take out his heart, but not always. It often happens that time won't permit to perpetrate that barbarous part of their inhuman cruelty. After all they cut round the top of the crown to the skull bone and, raising up one side of the skin with the knife, with a jerk they tear it off by the hair and the work is done; upon which they set up the Indian whoop as a signal to their barbarous companions that the work is finished, as also a shout of triumph.

The British soldiers, following four years of warfare in North America, had learned how to beat the Indians at their own game. They ambushed them in turn and scalped their victims with such ferocity that Wolfe found it necessary to forbid 'the inhuman practice of scalping except when the enemy are Indians or Canadians dressed like Indians'.

Unable to lure Montcalm out, Wolfe went in. It was just possible, he believed, to bypass the Montmorency gorge on the fordable mudflats where that river flowed into the St Lawrence, if at the same time the fleet bombarded the two French redoubts guarding the ford. The master of the frigate *Mercury*, James Cook, was sent to make soundings, reaching so close to the shore that he was nearly captured by Montcalm's Indians who paddled out in their canoes. Cook, the future circumnavigator, reported that the water was sufficiently deep to float a battleship. Admiral Saunders despatched the 64-gun *Centurion* to fire on the redoubts.

A Grenadier of the Lancashire Militia, one of the 'home-guard' mobilised by William Pitt to protect England against French invasion.

The attack was launched on 31 July. Townsend and Murray succeeded in crossing the ford and reached the beach below the redoubts. Wolfe watched from a flat-bottomed boat as the grenadiers, 'impatient to acquire glory' and without waiting for the bulk of the force to land as they had been ordered, charged up the cliffs and attempted to carry the redoubts. They became entangled in the glacis of trees and faced devastating fire. They ran back to the shore in disorder, having lost four hundred and fifty officers and men, killed or wounded. The retreat ordered by Wolfe was covered by the battleships. During the day they threw three thousand shells into the French fortifications, killing and wounding seventy of the defenders. Wolfe again criticised Townsend's dilatory behaviour, and he rebuked the grenadiers for their 'impetuous, irregular and unsoldier-like proceedings'. But the fault was Wolfe's; he had sent his troops to attack a numerically superior force protected by a position of enormous natural strength.

The assault was launched, states the diarist Captain Knox, against the advice of Wolfe's officers. Townsend was the chief malcontent. He employed his gift of caricature to discredit Wolfe, whom he depicted setting up lines of circumvallation round a brothel. He handed his drawing around the mess. Wolfe took the slight calmly: 'If we live this shall be enquired into, but we must first beat the enemy'.

Wolfe blamed himself for the failure to take Quebec. 'The enemy puts nothing to risk', he told his mother, and he could not in conscience put his army to risk. Wolfe did not know what to do next. The navy supplied the answer.

Chapter 8

The Plains of Abraham

The great bombardment of Quebec had begun on 12 July. It enabled Admiral Saunders to send ships to run the gauntlet and sail above the town, whose guns were now silenced. The French were completely unprepared for such a bold move. A curé remarked, 'The English are too cunning for us. And who would have expected it?' The navy's move, Saunders informed Pitt, 'gave General Wolfe an opportunity of reconnoitring close to the town, those ships having carried troops with them for that purpose'. Wolfe instructed Major Darling 'to look for places most convenient for troops to ascend at the landing on the northern shore'. Darling reported that he had noticed several places. Next day, 19 July, Wolfe joined the ships above Quebec. He made a reconnaissance with Admiral Charles Holmes who commanded the squadron, and as a result Wolfe instructed Brigadier Townsend to bring up his battalion. In his covering letter, Saunders told Townsend 'the general designs to make his attack above the town'. Wolfe immediately countermanded the order.

Wolfe's indecision led Townsend to remark, 'The general seemed to be at a standstill which place to make the attack'. Wolfe explained to Pitt why he had abandoned the idea, which he seems to have conceived suddenly, of landing troops on the northern bank above Quebec. He had found the French alert, and the nature of the ground unsuitable. 'But what I feared most was that if we should land between the town and Cap Rouge, the first body landed could not be reinforced before they were attacked by the enemy's whole army.' He went on to say that 'notwithstanding these difficulties', he thought of attempting a landing at St Michael's, a small settlement three miles above Quebec. 'But,' he continued, 'perceiving that the enemy, jealous [i.e. suspicious] of the design, were preparing against it, and had actually brought artillery and a mortar,' it seemed so hazardous that he thought it better to desist.

These documents show that in July Wolfe had in mind to make a landing above Quebec, a scheme which he appears to have abandoned completely, and revived only as a last resort. Montcalm also thought a landing above the town was impossible. Wolfe, he believed, intended only to 'give us some uneasiness', in order to 'displease us', meaning to cause the French to move their army, while he struck at the French camp between Beauport and the St Charles river. Wolfe's move up river was thus only a feint to distract attention from his true objective, the northern shore to the east

Opposite James Wolfe died at Quebec at the moment of victory. His body was taken on board H.M.S. *Lowestoft* and borne to England for burial in the family vault at Greenwich.

Admiral Charles Holmes, who commanded the fleet at Quebec.

of Quebec. Montcalm was correct in his assessment.

Holmes' move up river was more than a feint or reconnaissance. Wolfe had two secondary purposes, 'to divide the enemy' and force their attention as high up the river as possible, and 'to procure some intelligence'. The naval feat warned Montcalm of the threat to his supply line to Montreal; he detached Colonel Dumas with six hundred men to guard it. Colonel Carleton found them drawn up on the shore at Pointe aux Trembles, thirty miles above Quebec.

Wolfe's confidence that he could win Quebec easily had been badly shaken, and his next move may have derived from the tension from which he was suffering. He reversed his previous order, guaranteeing the safety of the French peasants as long as they remained neutral, and sent his troops looting and pillaging along the southern shore. 'Old people of seventy years and boys of fifteen,' Wolfe complained, 'fire at our detachments and kill and wound our men from the edge of the woods.' The wretched *habitants* were caught between two fires. The French militiamen hid in their villages to snipe at the British. They terrorised the population to resist the invaders. Wolfe warned them against 'misplaced obstinacy and imprudent valour': if they resisted the troops they could expect 'the utmost cruelty that war could offer'.

The smoke rising from the burning villages failed to move Montcalm, as did the destruction of Quebec. Between 12 July and

134

10 August three times as many shells fell on the city as had been fired into Louisbourg. Five hundred and thirty houses were destroyed. A deserter told Wolfe he 'wished the affair was over one way or the other, that his countrymen were all discontented and would either surrender or disperse and act a neutral part if it were not for the persuasions of their priests and the fear of being maltreated by the savages'.

The French Indians informed Montcalm that they intended to return to their villages. 'We have conquered the English, driven them away,' he expostulated. The chiefs pointed to the long line of battleships anchored in the river. Montcalm felt himself engaged in a lost cause: food was becoming scarce, and he was forced to weaken his army to allow the militiamen, or those who lived on the northern shore, to return home to harvest their crops. He sent fifteen hundred soldiers to Cap Rouge, eight miles west of Quebec, to strengthen Bougainville's force. Despite his pessimism, Montcalm thought himself safe as long as the campaigning season lasted, 'unless Wolfe lands above the town'. That seemed the last thing Wolfe intended.

Wolfe needed to learn what progress Amherst was making, and on 4 August he sent Brigadier James Murray to find out. He took twelve hundred soldiers up the St Lawrence with the intention of descending the Richelieu river to reach Lake Champlain. On the way, Murray also attempted a landing at Pointe aux Trembles. His soldiers were thrown back by Colonel Bougainville who had replaced Dumas. Murray attempted another landing further up the river with equal lack of success, other than the capture of some prisoners who supplied the required information. He returned to camp on 25 August with the news that forts Ticonderoga and Crown Point had fallen and that their garrisons had retreated to the Ile-aux-Noix on the Richelieu river. This information was confirmed on 4 September by two British officers who brought letters from Amherst dated 7 August. They had taken the circuitous and difficult route via the Kennebec and Chaudière rivers, made famous in 1775 by Benedict Arnold who used it to bring his army to besiege Quebec in the early days of the Revolutionary War. Wolfe now knew that he could not expect help from Amherst before the onset of winter compelled him to abandon the siege

To prepare for that eventuality, Wolfe thought to establish a camp on the Ile-aux-Coudres, down river, to house a winter garrison of three thousand soldiers. This idea was abandoned as was the desperate and hopeless attempt to storm Quebec directly across the river. The engineers reported that the ships of the fleet faced certain destruction from the city's powerful batteries.

Montcalm also received news of Amherst's progress, or lack of it. Bourlamaque, he believed, would prevent the British from reaching Montreal that year. The loss of fort Niagara posed a more serious threat: Montcalm sent Lévis to Montreal with eight hundred soldiers.

Wolfe fell sick on 20 August. His kidney complaint may have reached terminal stage. He roused himself to talk to his staff whom he told that he would cheerfully sacrifice a leg or an arm to take Quebec. He told his doctor that his illness was incurable, praying him to 'make me up so that I may be without pain for a few days and able to do my duty, that is all I want'. Wolfe's absence from the camp worried his soldiers. 'General Wolfe's health is very bad,' Townsend wrote his wife, adding 'his Generalship in my poor opinion is not a bit better, this only between us.' He said that Wolfe had not consulted his brigadiers.

From his sick-bed on 25 August, Wolfe wrote to his three brigadiers, begging them to meet and consult together 'for the public utility and advantage to consider the best means of attacking the enemy'. He outlined three possibilities; to attack the French across the Montmorency Gorge; to march inland in order to take the French camp in the rear; to assault the French camp simultaneously in front, left and rear, repeating on a larger scale the ill-fated attempt of 31 July.

The brigadiers in their reply rejected all Wolfe's proposals. They pointed out that should the army succeed in taking the French camp to the east of Quebec, it would still be faced by the impassable gorge of the St Charles river which protected Quebec on the east. They were unanimous in their opinion that:

The most probable method of striking an effectual blow is by bringing the troops to the south shore and directing our operations above the town. When we have established ourselves on the northern shore, of which there is very little doubt, M. de Montcalm must fight us upon our own terms. We are betwixt him and his provisions and betwixt him and the French army opposing General Amherst. If he gives us battle and we defeat him, Quebec must be ours, and which is more, all Canada must submit to His Majesty's Arms.

It has been concluded, from this document, that the three brigadiers, Monckton, Murray and Townsend, suggested the plan for which Wolfe has been given the credit. Wolfe thought no good could come of it. He told his mother, 'my antagonist has wisely shut himself up in inaccessible entrenchments, so that I cannot get at him without spilling a torrent of blood, and that, perhaps
to little purpose. The Marquis de Montcalm is at the head of a

A British soldier on
sentry duty at Quebec.

great number of bad soldiers and I am at the head of a small
number of good ones, that wish for nothing so much as to fight
him, but the wary old fellow avoids action, doubtful of the
behaviour of his army.'

Wolfe wrote in even gloomier terms to Pitt. He said, he had a
choice of difficulties 'that I own myself at a loss to determine'. He
knew that the affairs of Britain required the most vigorous measures, but 'the courage of a handful of brave men should be exerted 137

only when there is some hope of a favourable event'.

The brigadiers were confident they could get a footing on the northern shore:

There can be no difficulty to effectuate a landing in the night without the least loss, it may be done anywhere for the extent of a few leagues, viz from the height of St. John to Cap Rouge river. Two attempts may be made, either of which succeeding is sufficient.

The plan proposed by the brigadiers, to land well above Quebec, was not the plan Wolfe finally adopted.

The prospect of action, however doubtful the result, revived Wolfe. The plan, he told Admiral Saunders, was 'of too desperate a nature to order others to execute'. The two service chiefs discussed the operation. To Saunders Wolfe wrote: 'It will be necessary to run as many small craft as possible by the town with provisions and rum for six weeks for about five thousand, which is all I intend to take.' He thought he might find some opportunity to strike a blow, and hoped to 'have the strength to lead these men to where ever we can find the enemy'.

Wolfe withdrew his army from the camp on the northern shore, and on 3 September Holmes began the operation to pass Quebec with his twenty-two ships. He carried thirty-six hundred soldiers while Monckton and Townsend marched their men westwards along the southern shore.

These moves convinced Montcalm that Wolfe was making another feint to distract attention from his front, his camp at Beauport. He determined not to be fooled again into sending reinforcements above Quebec. He sought to recall some of the troops he had sent to aid Bougainville, but was restrained by de Vaudreuil. The Governor-General questioned which was the feint and which the real thing. Neither he nor Montcalm had any fear of danger at the possible landing places immediately above Quebec, for both officers were content that they were guarded only by militiamen. Montcalm instructed his officers to redouble their vigilance. On the night of 2 September, he wrote to Bourlamaque at the Ile-aux-Noix, 'the night is dark; it rains; our troops are in their tents with clothes on ready for alarm. I am in my boots, my horse saddled. In fact, this is my usual way. I wish you were here, for I cannot be everywhere, though I multiply myself and have not taken off my clothes since 23rd June.'

Although Montcalm commanded a numerically stronger army than Wolfe, only twenty-nine hundred of his men were regular soldiers. The militia, men between the ages of fifteen and seventy, made up the bulk of his army. Three thousand men were

Admiral Sir Edward
Hawke, the victor of
Quiberon Bay. *From the
portrait by Francis Cotes*

The Battle of Quiberon Bay, where Admiral Sir Edward Hawke crushed the French fleet, which had taken refuge in the bay on the Biscayan coast. *From the painting by Richard Paton*

stationed between Cap Rouge and Pointe aux Trembles, under the command of Bougainville. To him de Vaudreuil wrote on 5 September, 'I need not say to you that the safety of the Colony is in your hands. Certainly the plan of the enemy is to cut our communications by making disembarkations on the northern shore. Only vigilance can prevent it.'

Montcalm did not expect an actual invasion above Quebec. He withdrew from Bougainville the Guyenne regiment, thus reducing his force by a thousand soldiers. He told him, 'the most important point, my dear Bougainville, is to follow every move of the corps which you have on the water in front of you. You will thus be on the spot to deal with their disembarkation, even if you do not have all your people with you, but you should be able to contain them until your tail arrives.'

Montcalm thought that the British, by moving up river, intended only to cut his supply line in order to starve Quebec into surrender. The flower of the British army, he believed, still lay below the city. Wolfe, he told Bougainville, was playing a game of dice (a French game called *tope et tingue*) where, having played to the left, and then to the right, he would proceed to play the middle. By that he meant that Wolfe would attempt another frontal assault east of Quebec. But, he warned Bougainville, 'Mr Wolfe is just the man to double back in the night.'

In consequence of the conflicting advice he had received from the two commanders, Bougainville spread his depleted army thinly along the northern shore, between Pointe aux Trembles and the little cove named Anse des Mères, a mile and a half west of Quebec. The 180 foot high cliffs at that point were inaccessible, thought Montcalm. To de Vaudreuil's protest that they needed guarding, Montcalm replied, 'Only God, Sir, can do the impossible, we cannot believe that the enemy have wings that would allow them on one night to cross the water, land, climb rugged slopes and scale walls.' A hundred men posted above the cove would stop Wolfe's whole army.

The picket on the cliff above the cove was commanded by du Verger, the officer who three years before had surrendered Fort Beauséjour at the head of the Bay of Fundy, a dereliction of duty for which he had been court-martialled. Only his friendship with de Vaudreuil had saved him from conviction for cowardice. When Montcalm sought to remove du Verger, de Vaudreuil intervened and he stayed at his post.

During the early days of September, Wolfe withdrew his army from the camp by the Montmorency Falls to the southern shore.

The British troops
embark nine miles above
Quebec for the assault
which led to victory on
13 September 1759.

Montcalm found Wolfe's moves 'as embarrassing as they were
equivocal'. He still expected the attack to come at Beauport.
Wolfe's other moves were feints. Nonetheless, he had qualms
about denuding Bougainville's force. On 5 September, he sent
the Guyenne regiment to rejoin him.

When next day Holmes sailed his ships up river, Bougainville
immediately marched his soldiers along the river bank. On 7 September Holmes moved up to Pointe aux Trembles. Bougainville
came hurrying up, disclosing that he was under orders to follow the
British ships. During the next two days Holmes allowed his ships
to drift up and down with the tide. Bougainville marched his
men parallel with the ships until, unwilling to exhaust them further,
he rested them at Cap Rouge, convinced that he had been duped.

Strong winds and lashing rain, the foretaste of approaching
autumn, prevented action between 7 and 9 September. Wolfe took
the opportunity of enforced rest to write what proved to be his last
despatch. He addressed it to Lord Holdernesse, Pitt's co-Secretary
of State, and he wrote in gloomy vein:

We are now here with about 3,600 men waiting an opportunity to attack
them when and where they can best be got at. The weather has been
extremely unfavourable for a day or two, so that we have been inactive.

I am so far recovered as to do my business, but my constitution is entirely ruined, without the consolation of having done any considerable service to the State, or without any prospect of it.

Pitt received this letter on 14 October. He abandoned all hope of success.

Taking Holmes, Monckton, Townsend and Carleton, Wolfe landed on the southern shore where, disguised in soldiers' great-coats, the officers surveyed the opposite cliffs from a height. On the plain above the cove named Anse des Mères, they detected a small encampment of tents, sufficient to house a hundred men – du Verger's picket. From the cove a zig-zag path, the Foulon Pass, wound to the cliff top. The cliffs between the cove and Quebec, the Plains of Abraham, were bare of troops. Wolfe brought his officers back to the observation point on 11 September. He then disclosed his plan to ascend the cliff at the Foulon Pass and to do so at night.

Wolfe's selection of this cove may have been influenced, it has been suggested, by the advice of the Virginia Captain, Robert Stobo. His story is worth telling on its own account. He had sur-rendered with Washington at Fort Necessity and had been taken as a hostage to Fort Duquesne, where he was placed on parole. He stole a plan of the fort, which he managed to send to General Braddock. It was found in that General's chest after his defeat on the Monongahela, and traced to Stobo. He was condemned to death and transferred to Quebec, to await confirmation of his sentence from Paris. The laxity of his guards enabled Stobo to observe the city's defences. He succeeded in escaping and reached Louisbourg by canoe in April 1759. He joined Wolfe, to whom he may have given useful information.

Wolfe's determination to land at the cove evoked strong protest from the three brigadiers. Their remonstrance bordered on insub-ordination. Holmes doubted his ability to ferry troops at night through the cross currents. Writing after the event he called the operation 'the most hazardous and difficult task I was ever engaged in', due to the distance of the landing-place, the impetuosity of the tide, the darkness of the night and the great chance of exactly hitting the intended spot 'without discovery or alarm'. The whole operation had been extremely difficult and failing 'would have brought upon me an implication of being the cause of the miscarriage of the attack, and all the misfortune that might happen to the troops'.

The brigadiers preferred their own plan, to land further up the 143 river somewhere between Cap Rouge and Pointe aux Trembles, the plan which they believed that Wolfe had approved. 'This alteration of the Plan of Operations was not, I believe, approved by many, besides myself,' Holmes thought. Writing many years later to Townsend, Murray decried Wolfe's desertion 'of the sensible, well concerted, Enterprise, to land at the Pointe aux Trembles, where without opposition, with this whole army, and artillery, he might have taken post and entrenched himself between the army and their Provinces'. He called the landing at the Foulon Pass 'almost impossible'.

Wolfe peremptorily dismissed the objections raised by his officers. He backed up his verbal stricture by a formal letter:

I had the honour to inform you today that it is my duty to attack the French army. To the best of my knowledge and abilities I have fixed upon that spot where we can act with the most force, and are most likely to succeed. If I am mistaken, I am sorry for it, and must be answerable to His Majesty and the public for the consequences.

What Wolfe should or should not have done has been argued for two centuries. On the one hand it is said that he took an appalling risk. He proposed to land his army *between* Bougainville's strong force and Montcalm's main army. The two French generals needed only to converge to trap Wolfe's army, or such troops as had succeeded in scaling the cliff, between two fires. Wolfe would have avoided that danger by landing, as the brigadiers had proposed, between Cap Rouge and Pointe aux Trembles. Bougainville's force was too scattered to prevent a landing there. On the other hand, it is claimed that by thrusting into the gap between the two French armies, Wolfe performed a stroke of genius. And so, of course, events proved. Montcalm blundered, but with some excuse. He advanced to attack Wolfe without waiting for Bougainville to come up, in the reasonable expectation that the British could not have landed and taken more than a small force up the cliff in one night.

To prepare for the operation Wolfe ordered the troops, who were camped on the shore, to assemble on the beach at 5.00 o'clock in the morning of 12 September, in readiness to embark, land and attack the enemy.

During the day two French deserters from Bougainville's army brought news that a provision convoy would attempt to slip past the British ships and reach Quebec during the night of 12 September. This information was important for it implied that the French sentries on the river bank might mistake the British landing craft for the expected convoy.

Wolfe issued his final orders:

The enemy's force is now divided; great scarcity of provisions is in their camp, and universal discontent among the Canadians. The second officer in command is gone to Montreal, or St John's, which gives reason to think that General Amherst is advancing into the colony. A vigorous blow struck by the army at this juncture may determine the fate of Canada. Our troops below are in readiness to join us; all the light infantry and tools are embarked at Pointe Lévis, and the troops will land where the French seem least to expect it.

The first body that gets on shore is to march directly to the enemy, and drive them from any little post they may occupy. The officers must be careful that the succeeding bodies do not by any mistake fire upon those who go before them. The battalions must form on the upper ground with expedition, and be ready to charge whatever presents itself. When the artillery and troops are landed, a corps will be left to secure the landing-place, while the rest march on and endeavour to bring the French and Canadians to battle.

The officers and men will remember what their Country expects from them, and what a determined body of soldiers, enured to war, is capable of doing against five weak French battalions mingled with disorderly peasantry. The soldiers must be attentive and obedient to their officers, and the officers resolute in the execution of their duty.

The soldiers were not told where they would land. The regiments were formed into three brigades; each man carried his musket, food and rum for two days. They embarked at 9.00 p.m. Holmes allowed his ships to float up river on the tide, the landing-craft masked by the bulk of the three frigates and six smaller vessels. They turned at 2.00 a.m. and drifted down river again. Two lanterns hoisted on the main mast of the *Sunderland* signalled for the landing boats to cast off. To create a diversion Admiral Saunders moved his big ships across the Quebec basin towards the northern shore. They dropped anchors and buoys and commenced firing into the French lines on the cliffs east of Quebec. The soldiers stood to arms, expecting a landing.

Observing Holmes' ships in the bright moonlight, Bougainville concentrated his army at Pointe aux Trembles. When the ships drifted away he concluded that Holmes was up to his old tricks, aiming to tire his troops by keeping them marching up and down the river. Refusing to be duped again, Bougainville stayed where he was. The naval activity, however, led him to cancel the provision convoy. However, by some oversight the sentries along the river bank were not informed.

Montcalm, in his camp below Quebec, awaited events. When de Vaudreuil expressed the fear that the British might come ashore at L'Anse des Mères, and suggested increasing the patrol at that point, Montcalm laughed him to scorn, saying there were too

many men there already. One hundred men in that position would give ample time: 'we could wait for daylight and march there'.

The first wave of boats carried four hundred light infantrymen commanded by Colonel William Howe, and thirteen hundred other soldiers, Monckton and Murray's battalions. That was all the twenty-six boats could carry. When they had landed this advance force they would return to the battleships to embark the second wave, the 1,910 soldiers of Townsend's command. A further twelve hundred men were held in reserve.

Guided by the naval Captain Chads, the boats dropped gently down river, hugging the northern shore. Wolfe's boat carried the twenty-four light infantrymen destined to lead the landing. The midshipman in charge, John Robinson, overheard Wolfe softly reciting to the silent officers Gray's 'Elegy in a Country Church-yard'. Wolfe told them, 'Gentlemen, I would rather have written those lines than take Quebec'. Robinson particularly noticed the poet's last words, prophetic as it came to pass, 'The paths of glory

lead but to the grave'.

The path to glory nearly ended disastrously.

Ahead, in midstream, lay the sloop *Hunter*. Her commander knew that a French provision convoy was expected, but had not been told it would be preceded by Wolfe's boats. Spotting the boats, Lieutenant Smith ran out his guns and prepared to fire. Wolfe heard the noise and directed Robinson to turn his boat towards the sloop. He identified himself just in time. One danger had been averted, another loomed ahead.

The French had posted sentries on the beach below the village of Sillery, half a mile above the cove where Wolfe intended to land. The boats slipped past the first sentry unobserved. The second sentry was more alert. 'Qui vive?' he called. The soldiers in the boats tensed. Captain Donald McDonald rose to the occasion. He spoke perfect French. 'La France', he replied. The sentry was not completely reassured. 'Quel régiment?' he questioned. 'De Reine', called McDonald. That was one of the regiments commanded by Bougainville. His answer satisfied the sentry, but the danger was not yet over. Another sentry, who was more inquisitive,

Model of an invasion barge as used by Wolfe to carry his assault force to the cliffs below Quebec.

147

took up the cry. McDonald had his answer ready. Keeping his voice low, he told the man it was the provision convoy, entreating him not to make a noise, lest the English hear.

Captain Chads in the leading boat sought anxiously for the

James Wolfe leading the night attack on Quebec.

jutting rock, the landmark identifying Wolfe's Cove, as it is now called. The boats pulled into it at 4.00 a.m. The beach was deserted. Howe led his twenty-four picked men ashore. Above towered the 180-foot-high cliff. Up it zig-zagged the steep and

narrow path Wolfe had spotted from the southern shore. The French had made an attempt to block it with felled tree trunks and sharpened logs, though its natural difficulties seemed sufficient to discourage ascent. The path was no more than a series of ledges and cracks, sprouting stunted shrubs and trees. They provided handholds. Grasping the bushes, clutching the ledges, Howe's men scrambled upwards. More infantrymen and Highlanders followed them. Howe waited on the beach. He watched his men reach the cliff top and disappear to the left in the direction of the clump of trees sheltering the French tents.

Writing to Lord Anson after the event, Admiral Saunders reported, 'Considering the darkness of the night and the rapidity of the current, this was a very critical operation very properly and successfully concluded.' The taciturn Admiral could have bestowed even greater praise on his seamen, without whose efforts the daring landing could not have been accomplished. Saunders, no doubt in the highest tradition of the 'Silent Service', gave more praise to the soldiers, saying that the difficulty of scaling the cliff was 'scarcely credible'. Seldom can there have been greater understanding and co-operation between a military and a naval force.

The picket on the cliff-top heard nothing. Du Verger had given fifty of his men permission to return to their farms, where the harvest awaited reaping. The other fifty men were asleep in their tents. One sentry stood guard. McDonald employed his French again, and told the man he led reinforcements from Quebec. Howe's men rushed the encampment. The French militia, awakened suddenly, fired a few shots and fled through the woods. Du Verger was wounded and taken prisoner. An English 'huzza' told Wolfe that the objective had been gained. He and Monckton crawled up the cliff followed by the light infantrymen and Highlanders. Detachments were sent running along the cliff to silence the French posts. One post commenced firing. Did that signify the arrival of reinforcements? Wolfe was uncertain. He sent down a message warning Barré, who acted as Beach-Master, to delay the landing of the second wave of assault troops. Barré disregarded the order, fortunately as it turned out, for the French post was firing upon Holmes' ships floating down river. Barré sent the empty boats back to the ships. Within two hours, 4,828 men had reached the cliff top.

For the second time in his career Wolfe benefited from insubordination. The landing on Cape Breton had been achieved by the inspiration of three of his young officers. Wolfe's hesitation led Townsend to 'doubt (and with great reason) the success of the enterprise'.

Wolfe stood in considerable peril, his troops isolated on the cliff top a mile and a half above Quebec. He was caught between two fires, Bougainville to the west and Montcalm to the east. If they converged to attack, Wolfe's small force could face annihilation.

Wolfe drew up his army in battle array on the cliff top and sent scouts westwards to see if Bougainville was stirring. They returned to report no sign of movement from that direction. In front and to the right all was quiet.

The French were beginning to realise that Wolfe had stolen a march on them. At about 1.00 a.m. a great noise of barges had been heard in Quebec. The troops in the camp east of the city were hurried into their entrenchments. No notice was taken of the message from Quebec received in the camp about 3.00 a.m. that 'something had passed'. At daybreak the troops in the trenches at Beauport were sent back to their tents. They had hardly bedded down when a terrified Canadian appeared with the wild tale that the British had climbed the Foulon pass, surprised the picket, and were deployed upon the heights. He alone had escaped. He was taken to the Chevalier Casgrain, Montcalm's aide. Casgrain recorded the incident in his Journal: 'We knew so well how difficult it would be to penetrate our lines at that point – if it was defended – that we did not believe a word of the man's story; we thought he had been driven out of his senses by fear.' Montcalm, who had been roused, thought 'it is but a small party come to burn a few houses and retire'.

The increasing daylight disclosed the British tents standing on Pointe Lévis and sentries on duty as usual. The French returned to their rest, except Montcalm, who set off to investigate with another aide-de-camp, Johnstone, a one-time follower of Bonnie Prince Charlie. He rode to the St Charles river, crossed by the bridge of boats and surmounted the slope to the west. Two miles to the south-west the British army stood drawn up in line. The sight left him almost speechless. 'I see them where they have no business to be.' He thought it a serious state of affairs. Montcalm galloped to de Vaudreuil's headquarters. It was 6.30 a.m.

Wolfe had decided to challenge Montcalm. After a time, when no army came to meet him, Wolfe marched his men across the plateau in order to get between Quebec and the St Charles river. 151

He halted his army on the slope of a small ridge, which ran parallel to and about a mile from the city's fortifications, which were out of sight. Between the ridge, the Buttes à Neveu, and Quebec the ground was partly pasture and partly cultivated; it was called the Plains of Abraham after its one-time farmer, Abraham Martin.

Wolfe had left one regiment to guard the landing-place where the navy was occupied dragging guns on to the heights. He drew up his remaining soldiers, 3,111 men, in two lines, forty yards apart. Townsend's battalion took position on the left, Murray's in the centre and Monckton's on the right. A heavy shower fell. As the clouds passed over, fitful sunlight glinted on the soldiers' red coats, muskets and the claymores of the Highlanders. The army stood still and silent. There was no sign of the French.

At de Vaudreuil's headquarters, Montcalm learned that the Governor-General, on his own initiative, had ordered the troops in the camp at Beauport to remain where they were. Montcalm countermanded that order and sent his regular regiments marching across the St Charles river, with orders for the rest of the army to follow at once. Despite his own reconnaissance Montcalm was still convinced that Wolfe had landed only a weak force. 'We must give battle and crush them before mid-day,' he told his aide de camp. 'We cannot avoid a battle. The enemy is digging in and already has two pieces of cannon. If we give him time to establish himself, we shall never be able to attack with the few troops we have.'

Montcalm had about ten thousand men, but only twenty-nine hundred were regular soldiers. The rest were ill-trained militia, farmers and peasants. He sent a message to Bougainville, urging him to hurry, to attack Wolfe in the rear. But he did not wait for Bougainville's three thousand soldiers, the élite of the French army. 'Thinking he could win the victory alone', Montcalm gave the order for his army to advance. If he had delayed for two hours he and Bougainville could have caught Wolfe between two fires. Wolfe had accepted that fearful risk. He gambled on the superiority of his troops, his disciplined veterans.

The French advanced up the reverse slope of the Buttes à Neveu. Fifteen hundred Canadian marksmen and Indians crept up on the right, from the direction of the St Charles river, firing and sniping at Townsend's battalion. He despatched skirmishers to keep them at a distance. Montcalm's cannon, the three field pieces he had brought from Quebec, opened fire about eight o'clock, their shells and balls flying over the ridge. The British artillerymen, the number of their guns increasing as the navy brought them up, replied. The sailors, by superhuman effort, had managed to drag up the cliffs eight 24-pounders, six 6-pounders and four howitzers. Montcalm hoped the artillery duel would cause Bougainville to hurry.

The French came over the hill at 10.00 a.m., and poured down the slope in three dense groups. Carrying their muskets at the slope, the British soldiers moved forward fifty paces, narrowing the decreasing gap to one hundred and thirty yards.

Wolfe had taken position on the left, selecting that side so he could oversee both the battle front and the approach to the ridge from the St Charles river, from where French reinforcements were likely to come. Unlike his subordinate brigadiers, who were in full dress, Wolfe wore a simple officer's red uniform and did not even carry a sword. He walked across the front of the line, ordering his troops to load their muskets with two balls and to hold their fire until the enemy came within fifty yards, the effective range of the musket. A sniper's bullet struck Wolfe in the wrist. Borrowing a handkerchief he bound up the wound. Another bullet struck him in the groin. The wound was insufficient to stop his walk which brought him to the right of the line.

The French came down the slope in blind, disorderly charge, firing their muskets at extreme range, too far away to take effect on the steadfast British lines. Wolfe, conspicuous on the right, standing in front of his troops, waited until the enemy had reached within forty yards. 'Present! Fire!' he shouted, waving his un-damaged arm. Raising their muskets to their shoulders, his soldiers fired one tremendous volley. The long line blazed as one.

The cloud of white smoke slowly thinned. The Frenchmen lay in mangled heaps, swept away by the flying hail of bullets. Those behind wavered and recoiled. Writing his diary after the battle, Captain Knox recorded, 'Well might the French officers say they never opposed such a shock'. They believed that every ball took effect, and had never before experienced such disciplined and regular fire. The British second-line, stepping between the soldiers of the first-line, fired a second devastating volley.

Wolfe ordered a bayonet charge, leading his men himself. He had gone no more than ten yards when he was struck by a bullet in the chest. Two men, Lieutenant Brown and Private Henderson, saw him stagger and ran to aid him. 'Don't let the men see me fall', Wolfe told them. They supported him to the rear.

The battle had lasted less than ten minutes. Wielding bayonet and claymore, the exultant British soldiers turned the retreat into a rout. Montcalm tried to stem the flight, to rally his panic- 153 stricken soldiers. He was struck in the groin by a bullet. His aide carried him into Quebec where he was attended by a surgeon.

The French survivors managed to escape, either into Quebec or across the St Charles river. Wolfe was still alive. Hearing the cry, 'They run! They run!' he asked, 'Who run?' 'The enemy, Sir,' he was told. 'Send a regiment to cut their retreat across the St Charles river,' he managed to order. He turned on his side, murmuring with his last breath, 'Now God be praised, I die in peace.'

The log of the *Lowestoft*, anchored half a mile off-shore, recorded:

10.00 a.m.   General action.
11.00 a.m.   Was brought on board the corpse of General Wolfe.

Wolfe had won a great victory. The French had lost 500 killed and 350 wounded, the British only 55 killed and 585 wounded. Carleton, Barré and Monckton had been severely wounded. Townsend took over command. Bougainville arrived too late to influence the battle. Townsend reversed his lines to meet him. Realising the battle was lost, Bougainville retreated, leaving the British masters of the field.

De Vaudreuil sought Montcalm's advice. He could do one of three things, the dying General told him: fight again, retreat to Montreal, or surrender. He could not interfere. 'I have much business that must be attended to of greater moment than your ruined garrison and this wretched country. My time is short, therefore leave me.' Montcalm died in the early hours of the morning, and was buried in front of the high altar of the Ursuline convent in a hole ploughed up by a British shell.

De Vaudreuil sent to Montreal for Lévis to take command. Lévis, when he was told that Montcalm had refused to await Bougainville's arrival, shook his head in bewilderment. De Vaudreuil was less sympathetic. He attributed the defeat to Montcalm's 'boundless ambition'. Another officer commented that 'Never had so many errors been committed in one day'.

De Vaudreuil called a council of officers to whom he proposed that the army should attack the British again at dawn. He received no support, and it was agreed that the army should retreat to Montreal. The Town Governor of Quebec was ordered to hold out as long as provisions lasted. The city surrendered on 18 September, the same day as the remnants of the army linked up with Bougainville at Pointe aux Trembles.

Townsend's despatch reached London on 16 October, two days after Pitt had received Wolfe's despondent letter of 2 September.

Townsend expressed no regret for Wolfe's death, saying only that he had fallen in battle. The British people were awed by their hero's death, and wept that Wolfe had fallen in the hour of victory. Bonfires burned in every village, except at Westerham in Kent where Wolfe had been born, and at Blackheath where his mother mourned her son. His body was brought to England for burial in the family vault at Greenwich, and at Pitt's and the King's instigation a monument was erected to Wolfe in Westminster Abbey.

Britain that autumn was overwhelmed with victories. The Duke of Newcastle called the capture of Quebec, 'This great, glorious, and surprising event'. He had dismissed the chances of conquering Canada as 'chimerical'. The rejoicings were even greater in the North American colonies. 'Carthage had been destroyed.' Numerous pastors made that classical allusion. Several preachers dared to predict that within a century or two America would become a mighty Empire.

The practical British rejoiced that by the defeat of the French in North America, they had gained the monopoly of the Newfoundland fisheries, where forty-three million cod were caught each year.

The French retreated to Montreal; the British fleet returned to England. Murray garrisoned Quebec with seven thousand soldiers. The winter was particularly severe, the damaged houses provided poor shelter and, by April 1760, his effectives had been reduced to three thousand men. Lévis had double that number in Montreal, though only two thousand were regular soldiers. In April he put his army into boats and ferried them to Pointe aux Trembles. Having got them ashore, he advanced on Quebec, taking the same position as Wolfe had done in the previous September. Murray should have stayed within his defences where, protected by the city's walls and guns, he was safe. A British squadron was expected in May, when the St Lawrence would be clear of ice.

Murray adopted the bold but unwise course of marching out to challenge Lévis, an experienced and able general. It was 13 September in reverse. The British charged down the ridge, knee-deep in melting snow, and were lucky to regain the safety of Quebec with a loss of 259 men killed and 829 wounded. The French lost 193 killed and 640 wounded. Pitt, when on 17 June he learned of the reverse, feared a 'fatal catastrophe'. It would be difficult, he knew, to raise another expedition to recapture Quebec. The people were 155

The Marquis de Vaudreuil, Governor of French Canada.

becoming weary of the war and wanted peace. Horace Walpole thought that 'America is like a book one has read and done with, but here we are of a sudden reading our book backwards'.

Pitt's anxiety was short-lived. On 9 May the frigate *Lowestoft* was able to navigate the St Lawrence to Quebec. More ships followed, and on 15 May Lévis abandoned the siege. His hope, to see a French fleet, had been blighted. The fleet of thirty sail, which set out from Bordeaux on 14 April, had been scattered and most of its ships captured. He returned to Montreal, losing many of the militia on the way by desertion.

Amherst, who had wintered in New York, called upon the colonies for one final effort. The response from the southern colonies was poor: Pennsylvania 2,800 militiamen, Virginia 400, North Carolina 30. The Maryland Assembly cheerfully voted a thousand men, knowing well that the Legislative Council would veto their cost. The northern colonies were more enthusiastic:

Massachusetts provided 7,500, Connecticut 5,000, Rhode Island 1,000, New Hampshire 800, and New York 2,680. But their mobilisation was tardy, so that Amherst complained of Colonial 'sloth'. He entered the St Lawrence from Lake Ontario on 14 August, with 5,500 regulars and 4,300 Colonials. Colonel Haviland brought his contingent from Crown Point, reducing the Ile-aux-Noix on the way. Murray came from Quebec. By 6 September, Montreal was surrounded by 17,000 soldiers. Two days later de Vaudreuil capitulated. The war in North America was over. France retained only the colony of Louisiana.

The French officers were repatriated. De Vaudreuil retired in disgrace, Lévis became a Marshal of France, Bougainville transferred to the navy, winning fame as the explorer of the Pacific. The French *habitants* became British subjects, exchanging, some thought, one servitude for another. They remained loyal to the British Crown throughout the American Revolutionary War.

The American colonists benefited from the war in which they had played only a small part. No longer need they fear French aggression. The *Pennsylvania Gazette* declared that the war had been 'the means of national advantages to us beyond what our most sanguine hopes could flatter us with'. The colonists had 'trampled our enemies under our feet and risen up upon their ruins'. The fabulous resources of the North American continent, its immense riches, lay within their grasp. For this they had Pitt to thank.

Chapter 9

The Battle of Minden

British troops fought in only one pitched battle on the continent. The six squadrons of cavalry and nine companies of infantry sent to Germany in August 1758 had fallen under the command of Lord George Sackville. He was subordinate to Prince Ferdinand of Brunswick, who had succeeded to the command of the Army of Observation, made up of fifty-three thousand men drawn from Hanover, Hesse, Brunswick, Bückeburg and Saxe-Gotha. Ferdinand was the brother of the Duke of Brunswick, and a brother-in-law of Frederick the Great. His role in the war was important, particularly to Britain. His army protected Frederick's right flank, and Hanover, from French attack. Frederick was hard pressed in Thuringia, his army of a hundred and ten thousand men outnumbered two to one by the Austrians. Following his success in 1758, Ferdinand manoeuvred to hold two French armies, the Marquis de Contades with eighty thousand men on the Rhine, and the Duc de Broglie with twenty thousand in Hesse.

The French Marshals set out to drive a wedge between Ferdinand's army and the Weser, the river protecting Hanover. They and Ferdinand raced to secure the town of Minden, which controlled the passage of the Weser. The French won the race. De Broglie reached Minden on 9 July, summoning its garrison to surrender. Major-General Zastrow refused to submit without a fight, saying, 'I have guns, powder and soldiers and before I can think of capitulation all these must have vanished'. The French forced entrance, and by evening were in possession of the town, with an open road to Hanover. Broglie was joined by de Contades who, as senior Marshal, assumed command. Ferdinand took up position on the west bank of the Weser, north of Minden. The French position was very strong: the Weser protected their front, their left was covered by marshes. They could not be attacked with any prospect of success. De Contades had one problem, supply. Ferdinand had placed six thousand men across his lines of communication. De Contades decided to attack. He commanded a numerically superior army, and Ferdinand's men were exhausted from long marches, lying spread out in the plain to the north.

By his scattered dispositions Ferdinand tempted de Contades to leave his secure position. He knew exactly what de Contades had in mind. On 29 July the French Marshal had asked the Mayor of Minden to recommend a reliable messenger to carry an order to the Duc de Brissac who protected the French rear at Herford, 25 miles to the west. The man selected by the Major spoke German with a

Opposite Lord George Germaine, the one-time Lord George Sackville, who failed to distinguish himself at the Battle of Minden and who, in later life, lost the War of American Independence.

159

heavy Westphalian accent. De Contades addressed him through an interpreter, unaware that he also spoke English and French. De Contades ordered the man to take a pair of shoes to de Brissac and to ask him to send two thousand pairs in return. The Marshal explained to his staff that his orders were secreted in the pair of shoes. The man left on his errand. He hurried across the marsh to the village of Hille, and gave the despatch to Prince Ferdinand to read before carrying the shoes to Herford.

The despatch confirmed Ferdinand's guess that de Contades would cross the Weser to attack him. During the night of 31 July, French deserters reported that the enemy were moving. Ferdinand ordered his army to be ready, the cavalry by 1.00 a.m. and the infantry by 3.00 a.m. Lord George Sackville was still abed at six o'clock. He should have been with his cavalry in the village of Hahlen on the right of the allied line.

De Contades threw extra bridges across the river. Ahead lay passable ground, two thousand yards wide, the left covered by marshes. To advance on this narrow front de Contades reversed the usual tactics, placing his cavalry in the centre and his infantry on the flanks. The army was ordered to advance at dawn. De Contades fully expected to take Ferdinand by surprise, and indeed it seemed that he had done so.

A three-mile gap opened between Ferdinand's main army and his left, the detachment at the village of Todtenhausen commanded by General Wangenheim. De Contades sent de Broglie to drive a wedge through Ferdinand's lines, thus exposing his left flank, while his own army assaulted the allied right and centre. The last thing de Contades expected was to be attacked himself.

Ferdinand planned to seize the initiative, rather than await attack: he sought to fall on the French while they were in the act of deployment.

Opposite Map of the German campaign in the Seven Years War. The French advanced, de Broglie on the right, de Contades on the centre, his army led by fifty-five squadrons of cavalry, and followed by the infantry with thirty-four guns. The artillery opened fire at 5.00 a.m.

De Broglie's advance on Todtenhausen was obscured by a heavy storm of rain. It took Wangenheim by surprise. He got his guns into action; they brought the French advance to a halt. De Broglie galloped to de Contades to seek advice. But de Contades had problems of his own. Looking to his left, he saw that his cavalry was seriously threatened. From the woods on the left, behind the village of Hahlen, emerged red-coated soldiers, the British and Hanoverian infantry. The allied army was ready for action by 7.00 a.m., its

right resting on the villages of Hartum and Hahlen, its left touching the village of Stemmer. On the right of the line stood two British infantry brigades, protected by the fir-woods; ahead and to the right Prince Anhalt's Hanoverian brigades. Sixteen French battalions were advancing on Hahlen. They were followed by fifteen more and by thirty guns. Ahead trotted the French cavalry. Houses in the village of Hahlen caught fire, the flames fanned by the high wind. The heat held back the French, the smoke blinded them. Ferdinand galloped to the left, the storm-centre of the battle. The British infantry were well ahead of the line, coming under fire from the French artillery. Captain William Phillips, commanding the artillery, saw the danger. He brought up his heavy guns at the gallop, an unheard of feat in warfare. They quickly unlimbered and threw shells into the French artillery, quenching its fire. The red-coated soldiers emerged from the fir-woods and charged the French cavalry, seven thousand horse-men trotting forward in two lines. They carried no firearms, only swords. Either they charged, or they would be shot down. The Marquis de Castries led eleven squadrons forward at the gallop: the British and Hanoverian infantry, commanded by the Earl of Walde-grave, advanced in three lines. Each man would have time to fire one round before the cavalry were upon them. Then it would be bayonets against swords and momentum. They held their fire, waiting until the French were within ten paces. The volley smashed de Castries' squadrons, who reeled back. The infantry closed their ranks, reloaded and marched on, ready for the next shock. It came quickly. Twenty-two squadrons thundered down upon them. They were met by a second salvo, fired at point-blank range. 'I never thought to see a single line of infantry break through

162

three lines of cavalry ranked in order of battle and tumble them in ruin,' remarked de Contades.

De Contades sent his crack cavalry regiments, two thousand glittering horsemen, to envelop the advancing infantry. It was 9.00 a.m. and the crisis of the battle. For the third time the infantrymen met the charge in unwavering line. The cavalry reeled back, pounded by the artillery. The French centre disintegrated, their guns fell silent. It needed only the allied cavalry to turn panic into rout.

Ferdinand sent an order to Sackville to bring up the cavalry on the right and complete the destruction of the French. The message was carried by Captain Wintzingerode, who spoke French but little English. He told Sackville to form line and advance, repeating the order twice at Sackville's request. To make the meaning clearer Wintzingerode gesticulated, using English words, indicating that Sackville should advance to the left, between the trees, in order to reach the heath ahead. Sackville assumed that he was intended to go forward. He sent an officer to move the Saxe-Gotha regiment of foot that obstructed his way, and a second officer ahead to ascertain where were the infantry he was supposed to support.

Eight minutes later a second order was brought by Colonel Sir

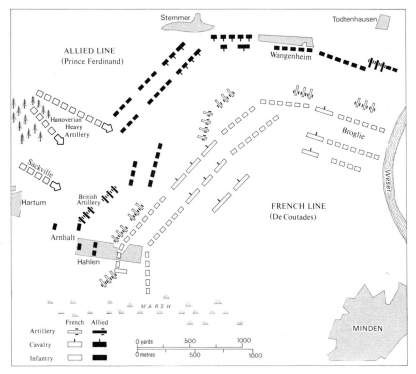

The Battle of Minden, 1 August 1759, at which Prince Ferdinand of Brunswick, Commander of the Allied Army, defeated the French and saved Hanover from invasion.

163

John Ligonier. It instructed Sackville to advance with the cavalry in order to profit from the disorder which appeared in the enemy's cavalry. Sackville put his cavalry in motion, advancing straight ahead. At this moment Colonel Fitzroy cantered up. He had met Wintzingerode returning from his mission and learned that the cavalry were expected to advance to the left. He told Sackville so, and that the wood on the left was more open than he thought. Nonetheless, Sackville refused to move. The cavalry remained behind the village of Hartum. Sackville rode to meet Ferdinand, asking what his various orders meant. 'My Lord,' replied Ferdinand, 'the opportunity is now passed.' In his absence the second-in-command, the Marquis of Granby, led the cavalry forward on his own responsibility. They were halted by Sackville on his return.

Ferdinand completed his junction with Wangenheim, closing the three-mile gap and forcing the French to retreat under the shelter of the guns of Minden. Had Sackville charged as ordered, claimed Ferdinand, the enemy would have been completely routed. As it was, they lost between seven and eleven thousand men, forty-three guns and seventeen standards. The Allies lost 2,600 killed and wounded, of whom 81 officers and 1,311 men belonged to the British infantry. The beaten French streamed through Minden and dispersed over the countryside without order or discipline. De Contades lost his baggage, including a number of letters from his government instructing him explicitly to burn and ravage without pity the German territories he passed through. Pitt published the whole correspondence, with infinite mischief to the French cause in Europe. By the end of the year Ferdinand had driven the French back to the Rhine.

Six British Regiments of Foot took part in the battle, the 12th (Suffolks), 20th (Lancashire Fusiliers), 23rd (Welsh Fusiliers), 25th (King's Own Scottish Borderers), 37th (Hampshires) and 51st (King's Own Yorkshire Light Infantry). Their successors carry the name MINDEN on their standards. On 1 August 1759, the Old 20th plucked roses and placed them in their hats, as still do the Lancashire Fusiliers on the anniversary of that day.

Ferdinand bestowed unstinting praise on his British troops, who had borne the brunt of the battle. On receiving his report King George commanded Sackville to return to England. In April 1760, a court-martial found him guilty of disobeying orders and adjudged him unfit to serve His Majesty in any capacity whatsoever, a sentence which George II declared to be worse than death. Whether Lord George Sackville was confused by his orders, or showed cowardice, has not been finally decided. He was lucky not to be shot like Byng. He had failed to make himself familiar with the ground, as all officers had been ordered on the day prior to the battle. Remarkably, even in that easy-going age, Sackville survived his disgrace. He was welcomed by George III on his accession, and, attaching himself to Lord North, became in time Secretary of State for the Colonies, when, by exercising that office, it is said that he 'lost the American Colonies'.

Sackville's command was taken over by Granby, who led the British contingent through the remainder of the campaign, becoming so famous a figure that to this day many English inns bear his name.

The allied victory at Minden saved Hanover and Brunswick from French invasion. Madame de Pompadour (honoured by one of her biographers with the title of *Général d'Armée*) called the horrible defeat at Minden 'the most melancholy check that we have received during the whole war'.

What had been gained at Minden seemed to have been lost in Prussia, where Frederick suffered overwhelming defeat on 12 August at Kunersdorff at the hands of the Austrians and Russians. It left him with only ten thousand soldiers. 'I have no resources more,' he lamented. All was lost. He awaited the *coup de grace.*

Political satire, 1759, on the Battle of Minden, depicting the controversy which surrounded the inaction of the British Cavalry commanded by Lord George Sackville.

The Miſtake a Satyrical Print on a late Battle near M-D-N in G-R-M-Y.

Chapter 10

Quiberon Bay

Choiseul recognized that France would lose Canada and her West Indian possessions. He planned to regain them by a master-stroke, by invading Britain and seizing several cities as hostages for their return. To achieve successful landings France needed to gain command of the sea, temporarily at least. The alliance with Austria provided a unique opportunity, for the French navy could now use the ports of the Netherlands. Their availability overcame the handicap from which all invaders suffered in the days of sail: the harbours on the southern coast of the English Channel were tidal and could not shelter fleets. But the use of Dunkirk and Nieuport was only part of the plan conceived by Marshal Belle-Isle. He proposed to land two armies in Britain. Fifty thousand soldiers would be transported across the North Sea in flat boats. Another army, twenty thousand men, would be conveyed from the Biscayan ports out into the Atlantic, round Ireland, to land in the Clyde. A third, smaller force, would make a diversionary raid on Ireland.

The plan was entirely beyond French capability of execution, for the French possessed neither the skill nor the resources to stage such complicated expeditions: the nation's Treasury was empty, her people discontented, her seamen untrained, her ships unmanned. Her naval strategy was based on the avoidance of battle, and to invade Britain her fleets would have to fight several battles. Choiseul hoped that the Toulon and Brest fleets could converge, collect the transports assembled in Quiberon Bay and slip out into the Atlantic unobserved. To transport fifty thousand soldiers across the North Sea, he needed to build 125 flat-bottomed boats in a dozen ports and bring them to the point of concentration. And France had to do those things under the watchful eyes of the British. Pitt refused to take the threat of invasion seriously.

He saw the plan's major defect: it was a soldiers' scheme to be executed by the navy. The French fleets would be clogged with transports, and having landed troops in the Clyde, would need to sail round Scotland to reach the North Sea in order to protect the passage of the flat-bottomed boats from the Netherlands. It would be an unwieldy operation, difficult enough for experienced seamen.

A letter written by Choiseul to the French ambassador in Sweden, intercepted by Newcastle's spies and smuggled to England, warned the British Cabinet. Newcastle agitated for the recall of the overseas expeditions. As usual he was timid and fearful, and his alarm increased in proportion to Pitt's confidence. The latter contemptuously dismissed the Duke's observation that the French plan was 'extremely well laid'. His gaiety infuriated his colleagues. Pitt refused to bring back a single regiment or a single ship, believing that the Channel and Mediterranean squadrons were sufficiently powerful to defeat both invasions. He dared not make too light of these threats, for he needed to persuade Parliament to call out the militia. When he spoke of the 'imminent danger of invasion' the Members of the House of Commons voted unanimously that they would:

Support the King with their lives and fortunes; his faithful Commons, with hearts warm with affection for His Majesty's sacred person and government, and animated by indignation at the daring designs of an enemy, whose fleet has hitherto shunned, in port, the terror of his navy, will cheerfully exert the utmost efforts to repel all insults, and effectually to enable His Majesty not only to disappoint the attempts of France but, by the blessing of God, to turn them to their own confusion.

Pitt relied on the people of Britain to mobilise for their own defence, but this was a factor on which he could not wholly depend. His Militia Bill, passed in 1757, had been abused. Men called up for home service had been drafted abroad, contrary to its provisions. Riots had resulted, and despite Pitt's assurances, suspicion remained. Several of his Cabinet colleagues disapproved of the Act and one, Lord Chancellor Hardwicke, instructed his son not to raise his county's militia. Politicians feared that the Act put too much power in the hands of the territorial magnates. Some householders refused to billet the militiamen, but the majority of the people responded to Pitt's spirit. As the year progressed and the danger mounted, fourteen thousand militiamen assembled in three camps, at Chatham, Winchester and Plymouth. Many towns and even individuals raised volunteer regiments, sufficient men to create eleven new infantry regiments and six regiments of dragoons. The mobilisation of these forces enabled Pitt to place the few regular soldiers remaining in Britain at strategic points.

Pitt relied on Lord Anson and the navy to destroy the French ships. Anson explained his strategy in these words:

Rear-Admiral George Rodney who captured Martinique in 1762.

The best defence for our colonies as well as our coasts is to have a squadron always to the Westwards as may in all probability either keep the French in port, or give them battle with advantage if they come out.

Anson sent Rear-Admiral Rodney to destroy the flat-bottomed boats being built at Le Havre. He sailed into the mouth of the Seine and bombarded the port for fifty-two hours, damaging installations and destroying a number of vessels. Two squadrons were placed to watch the ports in the Netherlands; Commodore William Boys cruised off Dunkirk, and Sir William Brett lay in

the Downs, the Kentish roadstead.

The conjunction of the French Toulon and Brest fleets presented the major threat. Anson sent Boscawen to the Mediterranean and Hawke to cruise off Brest to prevent these fleets from sailing or, if they succeeded in getting out, to destroy them.

Both Admirals adopted the new policy of close blockade. Previously the navy had relied on close watch by frigates, while the main fleets waited in the nearest port, in the Mediterranean at Gibraltar and in the Channel at Torbay near Plymouth. Close blockade in the days of sail was a difficult operation. While the in-shore squadron manoeuvred close to the port to be watched, the main fleet sailed up and down out of sight of land. The ships had to be victualled at sea and sent home in succession for repair. They could be driven off-station by gales and forced back to their home ports. The same gales would hold the French ships in their ports. There remained the danger, however, that the French might slip out when the wind moderated and before the blockading squadrons could reassemble.

Rear-Admiral Rodney, then a captain, commanding the British fleet which bombarded the French port of Le Havre where barges were being collected for the invasion of England.

169

During the summer Boscawen and Hawke kept watch, sometimes close inshore, on others refitting in their harbours. Tempestuous gales drove Hawke to seek refuge in Torbay. Fortunately, the French were not yet ready to break out. Admiral de Conflans took command at Brest in July, when he received this order from Choiseul:

If 50,000 men perish in a first expedition the King has determined to send out another force of equal strength, and we shall not give up as long as there are men in France.

This letter was also intercepted, copied and sent to Newcastle. Anson sent a despatch boat to warn Hawke who was off Brest. Pitt made no secret of the French invasion plans. 'We talk of nothing here but the French invasion,' wrote Lord Lyttleton from London.

In August, Admiral de la Clue sought to break out of Toulon in order to join de Conflans at Brest. Boscawen, badly in need of water and food, had returned to Gibraltar. De la Clue, leading twelve ships of the line and three frigates, skirted the North African coast, hoping to slip past Gibraltar unobserved. A British frigate sighted his squadron at nightfall on 16 August. Her captain signalled the alarm. Boscawen was ashore, his ships riding at anchor, their sails unfurled. Within three hours the fleet was at sea and in close pursuit of de la Clue who had got through the straits, though with loss of contact with his rear ships.

At 8.00 a.m. on 17 August the French look-outs reported eight ships to windward. De la Clue ordered his ships to lower their sails, thinking that his tardy vessels were catching up. More and more ships came over the horizon, eighteen in all. When de la Clue realised his error it was too late. He changed direction, ordering his fleet to make for the neutral port of Cadiz. One 'heavy-sailer', the *Souveraine*, delayed the escape of the others. Boscawen signalled for battle: 'the ships to engage as they came up, without regard for line of battle'.

The leading ship, the *Culloden*, blown by the freshening easterly wind, caught up with the rearmost French ship, the *Centaur*. Boscawen's flagship, the ninety-gun *Namur*, came into action at 4.00 p.m., losing her mizzen mast to the *Océan*. Even in this stricken state, the *Namur* was able to join the *Culloden* in pulverizing the *Centaur*. The French ship struck her colours only after her Captain had been wounded in eleven places and half her crew had been killed. Leaving the *Centaur* to her fate, de la Clue led his ships northwards, hoping to elude pursuit as darkness fell.

Boscawen caught up again at dawn, sighting the French ships huddled together in Lagos Bay on the Portuguese coast, close inshore. Rather than surrender, de la Clue ran his flagship on shore. He was followed by the *Redoubtable*. Two other ships sought safety under the fort's guns. Disregarding Portuguese neutrality, Boscawen led his ships in for the kill; they destroyed the *Océan* and the *Redoubtable*, boarding and capturing two other vessels. Of de la Clue's fleet, two ships of the line only reached Brest. The lagging rear-guard escaped into Cadiz, remaining there for months and finally returning to Toulon. The destruction of the French Mediterranean fleet enabled Boscawen to take his vessels to England, to add them to the Channel fleet.

The Duke of Newcastle heaved a sigh of relief. 'I own I was afraid of the invasion till now,' he admitted.

Hawke's blockade of Brest was broken several times by tempestuous gales, and his twenty-five ships of the line were forced to take shelter in Torbay. Each time he returned to his station off Ushant, to learn from the watching frigates that de Conflans was still in harbour. He was nothing like ready to sail. His ships lacked crews. This deficiency was partly overcome in late October when, during one of Hawke's absences, Admiral Bompar brought in his West Indian squadron. His ships were unfit for sea, and his seasoned crews were transferred to de Conflans' empty ships. On 14 October de la Clue received orders to take his twenty-one ships of the line one hundred miles to Quiberon Bay, where the troop transports were assembled. Hawke had been forced off station again, and on 14 November was sheltering in Torbay. The same wind blew de Conflans' fleet southwards.

It was spotted by a British frigate off Belle Ile. Her captain sent a cutter to meet Hawke at the rendezvous station off Ushant. He had sailed on the 14th and reached Ushant on the 17th, 'carrying', he told Anson, 'a press of sail all night with hard gales at south-south-west, in pursuit of the enemy'. He had no doubt he would catch up with de Conflans at sea or in Quiberon Bay.

The same frigate that had spotted de Conflans while on her way to England encountered Admiral Saunders off the Lizard, on his way home from Quebec. He decided at once to turn south to support Hawke; the news that de Conflans was out and Hawke was in pursuit electrified the British, and put even Newcastle in high spirits.

The gale that carried Hawke southwards had prevented de Conflans from entering Quiberon Bay. On the morning of 20 November his fleet was still twenty miles to the west of Belle Ile. At 8.00 a.m. the masts of Hawke's twenty-three ships of the line appeared over the horizon. The frigate *Maidstone* which was

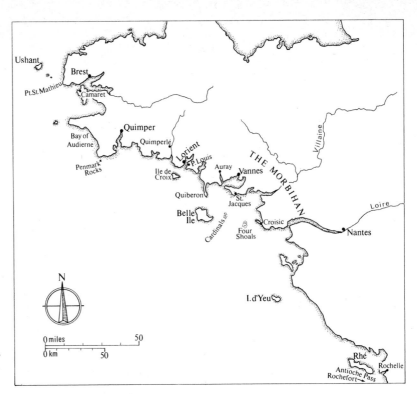

The west coast of
France, showing
Belle Ile and Quiberon.

leading the British van let her topsails fly, the signal for the discovery of a fleet. Hawke ordered general chase. De Conflans could
hardly believe his eyes, for he thought he had given Hawke the slip.

De Conflans sought to escape, to seek refuge in Quiberon Bay.
He calculated that Hawke would not dare to follow without pilots
through the tortuous, narrow passage between the Cardinal Rocks
and the Four Shoals. It was a chaos of breakers and pounding
surf: surely Hawke would not hurl his fleet upon a lee-shore
bristling with submerged rocks and uncharted reefs? De Conflans
got together his van and centre. His rear ships lagged, clustering
together at the bay's entrance.

Hawke came down on the wings of the rising gale, his ships
carrying full press of sail, shaking out their topsails. Keppel's
ship carried so much sail that the sea poured in through her lee
ports. Richard Howe led the attack in the *Magnanime*, pursuant to
Hawke's signal for general chase, for ship to attack ship as the fleet
came up. Hawke had no intention of being cheated of his prey. De
la Motte, de la Galissonière and des Gouttes had slipped out from
the British net. De Conflans would not escape. 'We crowded after
him with every sail our ships could bear,' Hawke told Anson.

172

De Conflans left the laggards to their fate. He hauled his ships round the Cardinals, leaving Rear-Admiral du Verger to take the brunt of the attack. The British ships descended upon his squadron like a pack of wolves. Nine vessels, the *Magnanime*, *Torbay*, *Dorsetshire*, *Resolution*, *Warspite*, *Swiftsure*, *Revenge*, *Montague* and *Defiance*, sailing 'in a close body but not formed in any line' swept by the *Formidable*, *Thésée*, *Héros* and *Superbe* pounding them with their broadsides. The *Revenge* and *Magnanime* engaged the *Formidable*, du Verger's flag-ship, quickly reducing her to a wreck.

Du Verger was wounded. He sat himself in a chair on the quarter-deck and remained there until he was killed, after which his brother took command until he also was killed. The *Formidable* struck at 4.30 p.m.

De Conflans tried to manoeuvre his van and centre within the narrow confines of the bay, in an attempt to sail out of the trap in which he had placed himself. A shift of wind confused the inexperienced French crews. 'When the van, in which I was,' stated one captain, 'tried to go about, part could not do it. We were in a funnel, all on top of each other, with rocks on one side and ships on the other.' De Conflans led his ships towards the outlet of the bay. His flagship, the *Soleil Royal*, was met by Hawke's *Royal George* off the Cardinals. Another vessel intervened, forcing them apart.

The *Torbay* fired her broadsides into the *Thésée*, both vessels rolling and pitching in the heavy seas with their gun-ports open. The French ship fell on her beam ends, filled with water and sank with the loss of all her six hundred crew. The *Torbay* nearly suffered the same fate.

The *Magnanime* and the *Chatham* engaged the *Héros*, raking her from stem to stern and killing every officer on board down to a midshipman together with her crew of four hundred, and forcing her to strike. Hawke tried to overhaul the French flagship, to prevent her escape. He ordered the Master to lay the *Royal George* alongside, a task he was loath to perform in the fading light and high seas. 'You have done your duty in this remonstrance,' Hawke told him, 'now obey orders and lay me alongside the French Admiral.' The flagship's action was prevented by the intervention of the *Intrépide*. Foiled of her prey, the *Royal George* poured her broadsides into the *Superbe* which foundered at once.

Hawke had stopped de Conflans' escape. Darkness was falling and the ships lay on a lee shore surrounded by foaming breakers, fanned by the high winds. 'Night was coming on,' Hawke reported to Anson, 'and being on a part of the coast of which we were totally ignorant, without a pilot, as was the greatest part of the squadron, 173 and blowing hard on a lee-shore, I made the signal to anchor.'

During the night two British ships, the *Resolution* and the *Essex*, ran aground on the Four Shoals and were lost. The French ship *Juste* sank in the mouth of the Loire, and the *Soleil Royal* and the *Héros* ran ashore, breaking their backs. At daybreak the eight ships of the French centre squadron made their escape from the bay, and reached Rochefort.

The French had lost six ships in battle: four more vessels went aground next day and became total wrecks. Even more serious was the loss of twenty-five hundred sailors, men who unlike ships could not be replaced.

Hawke had won a great victory. He had destroyed both the French fleet and the invasion threat, giving the French marine its *coup de grace*. He reported his victory to Lord Anson. 'When I consider the season of the year, the hard gales on the day of action, a flying enemy, the shortness of the day, and the coast they were on, I can boldly affirm that all that could possibly be done has been done. As to the loss we have sustained, let it be placed to the account of the necessity I was under of running all risks to break this strong force of the enemy. Had we had but two hours more daylight the whole had been totally destroyed or taken; for we were almost up with their van when night overtook us.'

Only the third French expedition succeeded in reaching Britain. The privateer Captain Thurot escaped with six small vessels from Dunkirk on 15 October. Early in 1760 he appeared before Londonderry and Belfast and landed at Carrickfergus where the garrison surrendered. However, on sailing down the Irish Sea Thurot was intercepted by British frigates, his ships taken and himself killed. The flat-bottomed boats never left harbour.

Hawke's great victory made a wonderful climax to the immortal year; the year of victories, Guadeloupe, Marie Galante, Ticonderoga, Crown Point, Niagara, Quebec, Minden, Lagos and now Quiberon. The *London Magazine* called 1759, 'A year as glorious as ever appeared, even in the glorious annals of this nation – for the glory of Great Britain may now be justly said to extend from the Southern to the Northern Pole – from the rising to the setting sun.'

Pitt was not satisfied. France must be crushed, never to rise again to pose a threat to Britain. He ordered the construction of ten new battleships, one of a hundred guns. How should she be named, enquired Lord Anson. 'The *Victory*', answered Pitt.

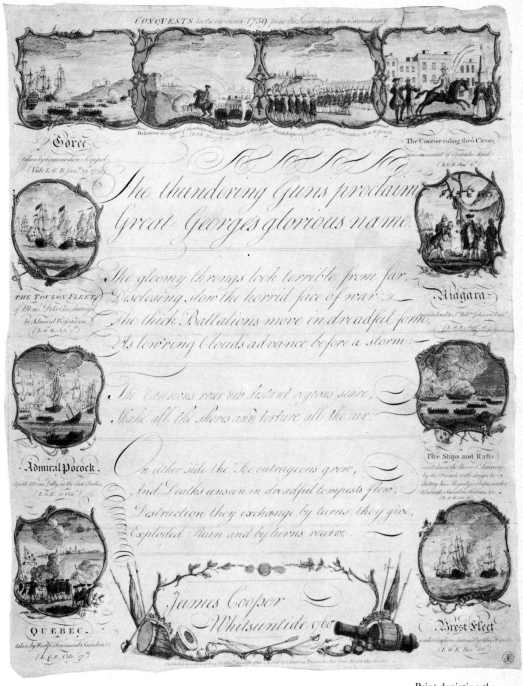

Print depicting the
Conquests of the
Glorious Year, 1759.

Chapter 11

The
New King

British predominance at sea in Pitt's war stemmed, not from the number of her ships or from their quality – they were inferior to French design – but from her experienced and daring seamen, men who knew their craft and were ready to fight. France lacked a similar seafaring population. Pitt believed that to make France for ever impotent at sea, it was only necessary to cut her off from her transatlantic fisheries, the nursery of the French marine. He was determined to deny France the overseas bases she hoped to regain with peace.

Thoughts of peace were stirring: the combatants were becoming war-weary. Britain had achieved her war-aim, the conquest of Canada. Prussia was exhausted, seeking a way out of the military impasse which was the consequence of her numerical inferiority. France was in economic collapse, incapable of recovery, and had nothing further to gain by pursuing Austria's quarrel with Prussia. Chief Minister Choiseul sought only to salvage something from the wreck of war. He planned to strengthen France's bargaining power by occupying Hanover.

Pitt wanted to finish the job by destroying France as a Colonial power. Cut off from world trade, she would stagnate and die, leaving Britain paramount outside Europe and powerful in international affairs. Pitt desired to carry the war to its logical conclusion, namely total victory. His policy carried the risk that the European nations would combine to thwart such a plan. To eighteenth-century rulers war was a game, to be played strictly according to the rules. Hereditary princes did not conquer their enemy. They fought to gain limited objectives.

The Duke of Bedford, an early ally and later critic of Pitt, expressed contemporary wisdom. The destruction of France as a sea-power 'must excite all the naval powers of Europe to enter into a confederacy against us'. British monopoly of sea power would be as dangerous to 'the liberties of Europe' as had been the military power of Louis XIV. It had 'drawn all Europe upon his back'. Bedford dreaded that Britain might overload herself with colonial possessions, as Spain had done to her ruin. He showed prophetic vision: 'I don't know whether the neighbourhood of the French to our North American colonies was not the greatest security for their dependence on the mother country.' He felt that dependence 'will be slighted by them when their apprehension of the French is removed'.

Antagonism to Pitt was mounting, the peace-party being led by the Duke of Newcastle. Only peace could rid him of the detested

Opposite Belle Ile, off the coast of France. The British made a successful landing in an unguarded cove near Locmarie Point.

domination of his overbearing colleague. Success had made the great war minister imperious, and he treated his ministerial colleagues with contemptuous disregard. His glory had made him enemies when he needed friends to help him persuade Parliament and the nation to accept the mounting burden of the war. Newcastle grumbled at its prodigious cost, particularly the subsidies paid to Frederick, who had achieved nothing. In fact, Britain had gained German help cheaply: her contribution to German victory amounted to £10,800,000, of which Frederick received £2,680,000. Britain's great victories had increased the national debt from £72 million in 1755 to £150 million in 1762. Britain's trade was thriving, while France's had sunk to zero.

Pitt's strength lay in his hold on the people, the inarticulate majority, few of whom were able to vote, though they, or the 'mob' as contemporary expression of popular opinion was called, could influence events. Richard Rigby, an observer of the scene, explained it thus: 'Mr. Pitt, it is plain, does govern, and the worst of it is, he governs not only in the Cabinet council, but in the opinions of the people too.' Rigby disparaged Pitt's victories, saying that 'fresh fuel is added to the delusion, and the fire is kept constantly fanned'.

Just when Pitt needed help, he lost the man who had become his chief supporter. On 25 October 1760 the old King died. The once hostile George II had learned to appreciate Pitt and glory in his achievements. He was succeeded by his twenty-three-year-old grandson, George III. The new King cared little for Hanover, 'that horrid Electorate', and was determined to rid Britain of the Whig oligarchy who had ruled for fifty years. Without Whig votes Pitt could not remain in office.

Pitt was given an early hint of the new threat to his power. On learning of George II's sudden death, he hurried to Kensington Palace to pay his respects to the new King. He was kept waiting for hours, kicking his heels in an ante-room. When, finally, he was admitted to the royal presence, George was making his accession declaration. He referred to the war as 'bloody and expensive'. The words were a direct challenge to Pitt's policy. He insisted that they be changed in the Privy Council Minute Book, to read, 'an expensive, but just and necessary war'. Further evidence of the King's antagonism came from his courtiers. They barely concealed their satisfaction at Frederick's complete rout in Saxony and the Austrian capture of Berlin. When the Protestant hero won a great victory at Torgau, they spoke disparagingly of the mob's 'indecent rejoicings'.

King George III, who, on his accession in 1760, was determined to terminate the war in which Britain had gained great victories.

   Pitt was forced to accept the King's favourite, his ex-tutor the Earl of Bute, a pompous and sly Scot, as his co-Secretary of State in place of the pliant Holdernesse. Bute and George III intrigued to get rid of Pitt, but they could not do without him as long as the war lasted.

   Public resentment of the continuing war was growing. It was expressed by the welcome given to the publication, in the autumn of 1760, of the pamphlet entitled *Considerations on the German War*, which went into six editions. Its author was a dissenting woollen draper who acted as London agent for the Colony of Massachusetts, named Isaac Maudit. He, or more probably Lord Chancellor Hardwicke who is believed to have been the motive force, concocted a clever piece of propaganda, and a powerful condemnation of Pitt's policy, by an ingenious distortion of his own long-abandoned arguments against military involvement on the Continent. Maudit criticised the folly of Britain, a country possessing a weak army and a powerful navy, engaging in a war between European nations, merely to ensure the safety of Hanover, the King's private domain. Maudit also sneered at the popular hero, Frederick, whom he portrayed as having set Europe aflame, sacrificing the lives of his subjects, and slaughtering his neighbours, all to satisfy his boundless ambition.

Maudit's arguments appealed to insular pride. Britain had gained all she had fought for. The policy of containing France in Europe had had no effect on the war for Empire, which had been won by sea power alone. Had France's military strength not been occupied in Europe, she could not have transported her soldiers overseas to defend her colonies.

Maudit's arguments were plausible, as Pitt knew. He had granted subsidies to Britain's allies and sent troops to fight in Europe to protect Hanover, to 'do the King's business', to secure his support for the greater war.

The pamphlet put Pitt much out of humour, thought his friend Sir Thomas Gray. His popularity was tottering. Horace Walpole, who had previously been in favour of the war, considered that many people had changed their opinion, because of the indecisive nature of the German campaigns. Even Pitt's most ardent supporter, the city Alderman William Beckford, jibed at Frederick, calling his last campaign 'languid'. The House of Commons resented the renewal of Frederick's subsidy. Pitt, declared Walpole, was lavishing 'the last treasures of his country with a prodigality beyond example and beyond excuse'.

Pitt was forced to make concessions, to terminate Britain's contribution to the Continental war which nonetheless he thought a 'right measure'. He did not believe that France was yet ready to discuss peace. Choiseul was engaged in a subtle game to bring Spain into the war.

Frederick lamented, 'everything is lost': he had no more resources and no hope of achieving final victory. In November 1759 he had suffered a heavy defeat at Maxen, and had lost Dresden, part of Saxony, Silesia and the whole of East Prussia. He was being squeezed to death by sheer weight of numbers, and his hollow victories, in August at Liegnitz and in November at Torgau, had failed to reverse the flowing tide. The coalition, France, Austria, Russia and the German Catholic Princes, prepared to crush Frederick and seize Hanover. The Electorate was still protected by the Army of Observation, commanded by Prince Ferdinand of Brunswick, to whom Pitt had sent reinforcements, bringing the

The Caribbean island of St Lucia fell to the British in 1762 without a blow, following the capture of Martinique, the chief French naval base by Admiral Rodney. Here Commodore Hervey's fleet is seen sailing into St Lucia. France recovered the island at the conclusion of peace.

total British commitment to twenty-five thousand soldiers.

Once again the French thrust across the Rhine, forcing Ferdinand to fall back. Although he had routed the French at Ziegenhagen and Warburg by the end of 1760, their armies lay stretched in an arc across western Germany. 1761 was a year of humiliation for both Ferdinand and Frederick: they barely held their own. The new year, however, brought a gleam of hope. On 5 January 1762 the Czarina Elizabeth died. The new Czar, Peter III, Frederick's fervent admirer, ended hostilities and sent the Russian army to aid him. This situation was not reversed by his assassination, for his wife and successor, Catherine II, enforced 'strict neutrality'. Seizing the opportunity provided by the disappearance of one of his enemies, Frederick struck at Austria, regaining Silesia. In western Germany Ferdinand forced the French to relinquish their hold on southern Hanover and to evacuate Hesse. He besieged and forced the surrender of Cassel, taking ten thousand French prisoners. These defeats blasted French hopes in Germany. They had suffered an even greater humiliation on their own coast.

Medal commemorating the Battle of Minden, the only Continental battle in which British troops fought.

Opposite page
A firework display in London to celebrate the Peace of Paris, 1763.

Pitt had struck a terrible blow at French pride. Fearing for Ferdinand and Frederick, and anxious to support them, he had proposed in the autumn of 1760 another diversion on the French coast, no less than the capture of Belle Ile, the island guarding the approach to Quiberon Bay and the Loire estuary. Belle Ile was the equivalent of the Isle of Wight which guarded Britain's naval base at Portsmouth. Pitt calculated that Belle Ile could be exchanged for Minorca.

The project was approved by the service chiefs and by Bute, who thought that Pitt should be allowed to run the war as long as it lasted. The laying aside of such a measure would be a blot upon the opening of the new King's reign. The old King's death delayed the start of the expedition until April 1761.

Commodore Keppel sailed from England with ten ships of the line and a hundred transports carrying seven thousand soldiers. They were commanded by General Studholme Hodgson, a veteran of the battle of Dettingen, who had served in the Rochefort expedition. Due to rumours of the 'prodigious armament', which had been preparing at Portsmouth, the French were ready to receive the invaders.

The French, Hodgson told Pitt, had fortified the whole island. Despite three separate landings, he had failed to achieve a foothold. The check was, however, only temporary. The fleet encircled the island, isolating its garrison. Following Wolfe's precedent, Hodgson

The Earl of Bute who succeeded Pitt as First Minister and who concluded the peace which gave away many of Pitt's conquests.

sought an inaccessible and consequently unguarded spot. He found it at Locmaria Point. His troops climbed the steep cliffs and spread across the island: the French retreated to their fort at Le Palais. Hodgson laid siege. A shell exploded the magazine, opening a breach 'sufficiently large', related a British officer, 'for a wagon to pass through'. By 14 June the sappers had undermined the scarp. The Frenchmen were allowed to march out with full honours of war, their drums beating and colours flying. They were transported to the mainland.

The capture of Belle Ile strengthened Pitt's hand in the peace negotiations, into which Britain and France had agreed to enter. There was even talk of calling a European congress to prepare a lasting settlement. Britain's position was further improved when news came of the fall of Pondicherry and the capture of Dominica. 'All is triumph. All is joy,' Pitt exclaimed.

Pitt was sceptical that the negotiations would lead to peace. He distrusted Choiseul, knowing from intercepted letters that the French minister was negotiating to bring Spain into the war, following the accession of Charles III who was not a friend of Britain like his predecessor Ferdinand VI. On 15 August 1761 the Bourbon kings entered into a Family Compact, in which a secret clause

The defeat of the French fleet in Quiberon Bay, 1759, by Sir Edward Hawke.

provided that Spain would declare war on Britain in May 1762. The Spaniards insisted on the delay to enable them to bring home the annual plate-fleet, the *flota* as it was called, from Peru and Mexico. These *flotas* carried a million pounds' worth of treasure, gold and silver ingots, jewels and minted coin.

Pitt insisted that Britain should issue an ultimatum to the truculent Spaniards, seize the initiative and capture the plate-fleet as it approached Spain. 'There was not an hour to be lost.' He demanded approval from his ministerial colleagues, adopting his most imperious manner. 'There was much altercation and thumping of fists on the table,' states Lord Chancellor Hardwicke: several ministers were so offended that they refused to attend further Cabinet meetings. Pitt waved under their noses yet another intercepted letter. It expressed Spanish fears that the *flota* might be intercepted by the British fleet. The city merchants supported Pitt, for there were rich prizes to be won in a war with Spain. Pitt ordered the reluctant Anson, now aged seventy and with his adventurous spirit declining, to send Commodore Keppel with sixty ships of the line to intercept the *flota*. Another fifty-four ships were available if required. Anson, in his youth, had captured the rich galleon *Nuestra Señora de Covadonga*, bound from Acapulco in 187

Mexico to Manila. It carried more than a million pesos of coin and 35,682 ounces of virgin gold.

The Earl of Bute, who was supported by the Lord President of the Council, Lord Granville, called Pitt's scheme 'rash and inadvisable'. His opposition precipitated a Cabinet crisis. Pitt insisted that 'Spain is France, and France is Spain': there was now but one House of Bourbon. The peace-party argued that it would be madness to rush into a new war before the old one was finished.

The Cabinet met again on 17 September, and arguments waxed so hot that the meeting had to be adjourned, reassembling on the twenty-first. The opposition to his scheme made Pitt even more intransigent, and when opinion went against him he insisted that the record of the vote should be sent to the King, so that the whole country would know who was responsible. He lodged his own protest. The minutes of the proceedings stated that Pitt's proposal had been rejected by the majority as 'inexpedient and unjustified'.

Another intercepted letter proved him correct. Spain and France had ratified their treaty: Choiseul's promise of peace was a blind, a delaying action. Still, however, the opposition stood firm. Afraid as they were to face war without Pitt's guidance, they were more afraid of starting another war in the same disastrous way in which the current war had opened. Boscawen had done too much or too little: Keppel might fail to capture the *flota*. The Cabinet agreed only that naval preparations should proceed as if war with Spain were certain.

Pitt appealed to the King, but with Bute lurking at his side, George III refused to accept his advice. The Cabinet met again, and Pitt reviewed the war in which he had led Britain to victory. Success had come from instant action; he declared that he would run the war his own way or not at all, and he submitted a memorandum setting out his arguments for instant war against Spain. Yet another intercepted letter seemed to suggest that the Spaniards were vacillating. The British plenipotentiary in Paris reported that Choiseul was anxious for peace and 'that the affairs of Spain should not prevent it'. The Family Compact might not be implemented.

Pitt asserted that Choiseul was bluffing, seeking to gain time while the Spaniards prepared. His suggestion that an appeal be made to the people was rejected; it was far too dangerous, for the British people would support Pitt. Each minister went separately to the King to state his case: Pitt also demanded an audience, though he only increased the King's antipathy. 'The King,' recorded the Duke of Newcastle, 'seems every day more offended with Mr. Pitt, and plainly wants to get rid of him at all events.'

The British plenipotentiary returned to London, and took Pitt's side. Spain, he thought, meant to declare war. His statement shook, but did not change, the peace-party's opinion. They stood their ground. Lord Ligonier, the head of the army, argued that war with Spain would add sixty thousand troops to Britain's foes. Anson declared that his fleet was not ready for action, that many ships had been too long at sea and were foul. Pitt's chief supporter, Lord Temple, left the room in a tantrum. Pitt refused to change his opinion. 'Being responsible I *will* direct, and will be responsible for nothing that I do not direct', he declared.

Pitt had raised a constitutional issue. Lord Granville, a previous foreign minister, explained it to his colleagues. If Pitt was resolved to 'assume the right of addressing his Majesty and directing the operations of war, to what purpose are we called to this Council?' However much Pitt might have convinced himself of his own infallibility, 'it still remains that we should be equally convinced before we can resign our understandings to his direction, or join with him in the measures he proposes'. Pitt, he said, 'is determined to leave us, since otherwise he would have compelled us to leave him'.

Granville was saying that no one minister, however triumphant, could appeal to the King over the Cabinet's head. It was a revolutionary principle in a period when the Cabinet did not acknowledge corporate responsibility for its actions. Granville meant that the King's ministers must reject the dictator, the individual who claimed to be wiser than the majority.

Pitt had lost the support of the colleagues who, often timorously and sometimes grudgingly, had allowed him to run his war his own way. They controlled the votes that kept Pitt in office. Lacking their support, he must resign, which he did on 2 October.

Under Pitt's direction Britain's armies and fleets had triumphed. His success, however, had led him into fatal error. He saw Britain as sole mistress of the seas. He would forestall and crush Spain as he had defeated France. He had broken the rule of the club, that no European nation should be allowed to become all-powerful. Louis XIV had been taught that lesson; Napoleon, Kaiser Wilhelm and Hitler would also learn it. Pitt had to be humbled. Richard Digby, a friend of Bedford's, called Pitt's determination to extract the full fruits of victory, 'the madness of the times'.

Pitt had stood firm on one issue, to strike at Spain before Spain attacked Britain. He was convinced that war with Spain was inevitable, and contemptuously dismissed the Spaniards as weak and unprepared for war.

Chapter 12

The
Moderate Peace

The Spaniards brought their immensely rich plate-fleet safely home in October 1761. On 18 January they declared war on Britain as Pitt had predicted. Pitt no longer controlled the war, but he had established the principles by which it should be waged. Britain was ready to deal Spain a crushing blow. The government, fearing Pitt's censure if they hesitated, acted at once. A great expedition was prepared to invade Cuba and capture Havana, the long inviolate symbol of Spanish colonial power. Pitt had prepared the operation with Lord Anson. It was based on a novel idea which had been prepared by Admiral Sir Charles Knowles, who while Governor of Jamaica had visited Havana and been entertained by the Spanish Governor. The Spaniards, Knowles reported, would expect attack from a fleet coming from Jamaica, through the Yucatan Channel and rounding Cuba's western point. The concentration of a fleet in Jamaica would give ample warning: no fleet, no invasion. The absence of a fleet there would lull the Spaniards into a false sense of security.

The fleet, suggested Knowles, should approach Havana from the east, sailing from the Leeward Islands, north of San Domingo and via the Old Bahama Channel. No sane seaman, the Spaniards thought, would hazard the dangers of that passage which was strewn with submerged rocks and razor-sharp reefs. The Spaniards had not used it for two hundred years, since it had become the graveyard of numerous rich galleons. Knowles' idea appealed to Anson, who possessed an ancient Spanish chart of the Bahama Channel, the booty of his youth.

Command of the fleet was given to Sir George Pocock, who had done so well in India. With Boscawen dead and Hawke occupied off Brest, Pocock's selection was an excellent choice. Not so happy was the appointment of the Earl of Albemarle to lead the fourteen thousand soldiers. Aged forty, he was a parade-ground officer, a friend of the Duke of Cumberland (he had been restored to favour on the accession of his nephew), whom he served as Lord of the Bedchamber. Two of Albemarle's brothers joined the expedition: Commodore Augustus Keppel acted as second-in-command to Pocock, while William Keppel held the rank of general. The military inexperience of the two Keppel brothers was partly overcome by the addition of Colonels Howe and Carleton, who had distinguished themselves at Quebec. Amherst sent two thousand of his veterans to support the invasion.

Convoying thirty transports, Pocock reached Martinique (recently captured by Admiral Rodney) in April. Pocock was told

Opposite The Spanish city of Havana captured by the British in the later stages of the war.

that the Spaniards had twenty ships of the line at Havana and that a French squadron was expected from Brest. In truth there were only twelve warships at Havana, and the Brest fleet had failed to elude Hawke. Pocock, following Knowles' route, sailed north of San Domingo (the modern Haiti), past the island of Tortuga, the famous buccaneer stronghold, into the Windward Passage where he was joined by nine ships of the line from Jamaica. Leading two hundred ships, he sailed cautiously into the Old Bahama Channel. Captain Elphinstone, in the frigate *Richmond*, preceded the fleet, checking Anson's chart (which he found correct), buoying the channel and lighting fires on dangerous reefs to guide the fleet at night. By 5 June Pocock was within a hundred miles of Havana.

The Spaniards in Cuba went about their business in blind security. Nothing could shake the Captain-General's complacency; not even the arrival of an excited merchant-ship's captain who correctly reported the British plan; not even the news brought by an officer who reported a host of sail out to sea. He was reprimanded for spreading false alarm and told that the ships were nothing more than the regular British homeward-bound Jamaica convoy. Pocock's huge armada hove over the horizon on 6 June. He had achieved complete surprise.

Albemarle threw away the advantage that had been so easily and brilliantly gained.

Havana was protected by the Morro Castle, the fort which guarded the entrance to the city's fine, natural harbour. Its heavy guns could destroy any fleet which attempted to bypass it. For centuries the Spaniards had expected attack from the sea; they had failed to fortify the low ridge which dominated the Morro Castle on the east. The occupation of this Cabana ridge by an invading army would render Havana untenable.

Pocock anchored his fleet eighteen miles east of Havana, and Albemarle landed his army. Pocock then sailed his fleet to blockade the harbour. In his report Knowles had directed attention to the Cabana ridge, Havana's weak point, saying that the guns of Morro Castle could not enfilade the ridge. Albemarle thought otherwise. Instead of assaulting the weakly-held ridge, he advanced his army to lay siege to the Castle. Commenting on the history of the operations, Knowles pointed out, 'Experience in former expeditions might have taught them that whatever is to be effected in the West Indies must be done as expeditiously as possible'. Knowles had warned of the danger that in Cuba's sticky summer heat, an army could quickly become decimated by disease. Pitt had seen this too,

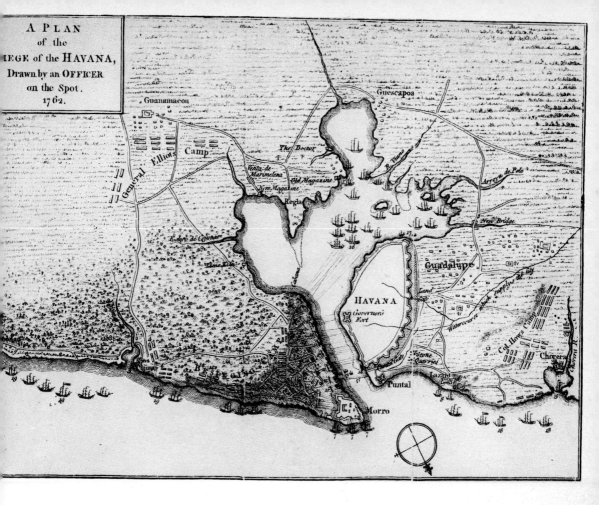

A PLAN of the ßIEGE of the HAVANA, Drawn by an OFFICER on the Spot. 1762.

and it was one of the reasons he had advocated an earlier attack on Havana.

Trained in the traditional school of European warfare, Albemarle saw no alternative to besieging the Morro Castle. It would have been easy to land part of his army to the west of Havana. The city, defended by only three thousand soldiers, would have fallen quickly. The ability of the British fleet to move at will gave the army complete mobility, and as Knowles had pointed out, 'unlimited power in an enemy's country during the continuance of a war'.

Two weeks (under the broiling June sun) were required for the engineers to construct batteries. They opened fire on the Morro Castle on 1 July: Captain Hervey brought in three ships of the line in an attempt to silence the Castle's batteries. The leading ship turned away, unable to face their fire; her Captain was afterwards cashiered. Hervey ran his ship aground, 'but my guns bear', he reported. He promised to stay as long as he could, despite the damage inflicted on his ship. When the smoke cleared, he hoped to see the army advancing to assault the fort.

Havana harbour and city, 1759, shows the British siege lines west of the Morro Castle which was also bombarded by the Royal Navy.

193

Albemarle contented himself with artillery fire; the gunners succeeded in dismounting some of the Morro's land-side batteries. Meanwhile Hervey's ships suffered two hundred casualties and considerable damage.

The Commander of the Morro Castle was as courageous as

The Siege of Havana, 1762. The English battery which bombarded the Morro Castle.

Albemarle was timid, and the six weeks' siege made Don Luis Vicente de Velasco famous. His three hundred and fifty soldiers, fifty seamen and fifty gunners were outnumbered by thousands: his bastions were battered from land and sea. The British naval gunners had landed heavy guns, and the way they handled them

The capture of Havana, 1762.

astonished the soldiers. 'Our sea folks began a new kind of fire unknown, or, at all events, unpractised by artillery people. The greatest fire from one piece of cannon is reckoned by them from eighty to ninety times in twenty-four hours, but our people went on the sea system, firing extremely quick and with the best direction ever seen, and in sixteen hours fired their guns one hundred and forty-nine times.'

Three weeks' bombardment reduced the walls of the Castle to ruins. No attempt had been made to isolate the Morro from the city, and it was periodically reinforced and relieved. De Velasco was seriously wounded, but continued to direct the defence from his hospital bed. The British engineers ran a sap along the edge of the sea towards the outward bastion which was protected by a seventy-foot-deep ditch. It could be crossed only by the narrow ridge protecting it from the sea. A sergeant and two soldiers crossed the ditch and scaled the wall: they found the guard asleep. No one came to support them so they returned the way they had come. De Velasco ordered a sally, but his soldiers proved no match for Britain's seasoned veterans. The engineers made ready to fire their mines.

De Velasco despatched a messenger to the Captain-General,

asking for orders. He sent his reply that the fort's Commander should act as he saw fit. De Velasco interpreted the order as condemnation to death; he must defend the Morro to the last. The British chose the hour of siesta to launch their final attack. At 1.00 p.m. on 14 August the walls of the Morro Castle collapsed under a terrific explosion. De Velasco rushed to the ramparts, and was shot in the breast by the soldiers leading the assault force.

De Velasco's achievement appeared to the British greater than their own. An officer carried him across the harbour, under a flag of truce, to be treated by the Spanish surgeons. He had been ordered to bring the wounded man back if he was unable to land so 'that he might be treated with all the care and homage that was due to an officer who, with so much glory, had known how to uphold his trust and the honour of his Prince's arms'. Inevitably de Velasco died, and when he heard of his officer's heroic death, the Spanish King decreed that a ship of the navy should for ever bear his name.

The British quickly occupied Havana, whose siege had cost the lives of eighteen hundred soldiers and sailors. In the next few weeks four thousand men died from disease, and hundreds more returned home incapacitated for life. The loot of Havana was enormous. One hundred merchant ships were found in the harbour and nine warships (one-fifth of Spain's navy) were captured. Vast stores of merchandise fell into British hands, three-quarters of a million pounds being distributed in prize-money. Pocock and Albemarle received £122,000 each; the two Keppel brothers divided £150,000. Each soldier was paid £4-1-8½d; each sailor £3-14-9¾d.

The loss of Havana was the first blow to Spanish pride. No longer could they assemble their plate-ships there for the voyage home. The British sprang a surprise attack on Manila, the capital of the Philippines and another source of Spanish wealth. Colonel William Draper was sent to India to organise the expedition he had suggested. He reached Madras on 27 June and sailed again on 29 July, with fifteen ships carrying 974 soldiers, all that could be spared. The flotilla sailed into Manila bay on 22 September. The Spaniards did not know that war had been declared, and while they argued what to do, the great annual galleon bearing the Mexican treasure came in and was secured by the British. The Spaniards refused the demand to surrender.

Draper, determined to storm the city, landed his troops while Admiral Samuel Cornish fired his frigate's broadsides into the Spanish soldiers who had assembled to oppose the landing. Next day Draper occupied the city's abandoned outer forts. Operations were halted by the breaking of the monsoon, but recommenced a month later on 28 September. A Spanish sortie was driven back and another summons to surrender was refused. It was impossible to storm Manila with the few troops available. Each day, as the siege progressed, the eight hundred Spanish soldiers were reinforced by numbers of fierce natives who entered by the distant gates.

Draper decided to storm one bastion, the 'Royal Gate', as it was called. It was protected by a wet-fosse, a covered way and a glacis, and the fortifications bristled with cannon. The navy landed its heaviest guns, which commenced firing on 3 October. Within a few hours they had silenced the Spanish guns and opened up the bastion. The Spanish Commander sent one thousand Filipinos, armed with bows and lances, pouring through the gate. They attacked the gunners with reckless fury, and dislodged and threw back the guarding Sepoys. But Draper's regular soldiers halted the charge. The natives, their morale shattered, withdrew. With the way ahead once more clear, the soldiers then charged the gate, putting its Spanish defenders to the sword. The Governor retired to the Citadel, where he surrendered. He was allowed to ransom the city for four million Spanish dollars, but alas, the soldiers' and sailors' dreams of riches were shattered. The Spanish government refused to pay the ransom.

Another British expedition captured Buenos Aires later in 1762. The project to seize Louisiana, the remaining French settlement in North America, had to be abandoned, due to the high mortality suffered by Albemarle's troops. Meanwhile the French, with remarkable enterprise, had raided Newfoundland, as Pitt had feared. His advice to reinforce the navy in American waters had been ignored by the new ministers, and the French did considerable damage before they were driven off.

The Spaniards had embarked on an even more suicidal enterprise. Following their declaration of war, they threatened Britain's oldest ally, Portugal, 'join us or be invaded'. The Spaniards commenced their shameless violation of neutral territory in May 1762. The Portuguese were in a parlous state; in 1756 Lisbon had been shattered by an earthquake which had taken thirty thousand lives. Britain sent an expeditionary force of six thousand soldiers commanded by Lord Loudon, whose wise caution had caused his recall from America. The Spaniards' three-pronged drive on Lisbon bogged down. The British counter-attack was led by a spirited
young cavalryman who routed a Spanish regiment, capturing

three standards and the regimental pay chest. Twenty-five years later the same General John Burgoyne surrendered to the Americans at Saratoga.

Spain had suffered yet another humiliation. On the oceans her merchant ships fell victims to British raiders. Choiseul sought to repair the damage, and once again planned to invade England, this time in conjunction with the Spanish navy. The allied fleets, sailing from the Mediterranean and the Biscayan ports, would combine to 'command the Channel', and secure 'a superiority in that sea for at least five weeks'. Together the two navies could amass fifty-two ships of the line in European waters, sufficient to overwhelm the British Home Fleet. Another thirty warships were available in the Caribbean to recapture Martinique and Guadeloupe. In order to disorganise the British defence system, the Spaniards were instructed to besiege Gibraltar. Fearing Spanish over-enthusiasm, Choiseul warned his allies that in spite of the wide distribution of their fleet, the British had throughout the war 'always shown themselves in a position to face every danger'. He exhorted the greatest secrecy. The invasion army, he told the Spaniards, would collect in small numbers in several scattered ports. The fleets would rendezvous at Ferrol.

Choiseul's plan suffered from excessive subtlety, and was beyond the naval capabilities of either France or Spain. Admiral Saunders prevented the allied fleets from leaving the Mediterranean; Hawke bottled up the French in Brest. During these operations, the navy gained the most notable prize of the war, the treasure galleon *Hermione*, sailing direct from Lima. She provided half a million pounds in prize money, and twenty waggons were required on 12 August to carry the booty through London to the Tower. The cortège was escorted by the Dragoons, and was accompanied by martial music, 'amidst acclamations of a prodigious concourse of people'.

The invasion plan was Choiseul's last throw. France had lost the war, having suffered one humiliation after another. Her navy had been shattered, her merchant marines bottled up in port. She had lost Canada, her West Indian possessions, her factories in West Africa and India, and Belle Ile on her own coast. Minorca had been her only gain. The French Treasury was loaded with debt. France was in a poor position to bargain.

Choiseul had feared to negotiate peace with Pitt, feeling he would rather be condemned to row in the galleys. But for Spain's entry into the war, and British vacillation, he would have been compelled to accept peace on Pitt's terms. Pitt would have dictated peace terms as a conqueror, but his successor, Bute, was in a hurry to end the war.

Pitt had retired into private life. Proud, unbending and loyal to the throne, he did not wish to embarrass the new government. He merely defended his own policies. To public surprise and dismay he accepted an annual pension of £3,000 and a peerage for the sake of his wife, who took the title of Lady Chatham. The people thought that their idol had sold his honour and his convictions to the men in power, and they dubbed Hester 'Lady Cheet' am'. Pitt's city friends declared that had they known of his poverty, they would have raised £500,000 by subscription.

Pitt made a dignified reply to the public's reproach. He begged people not to be too hasty in their judgment. He had accepted the King's pension as a reward for past services, not as a bribe for silence, and would not betray the people or the country. He asked his critics not to withdraw too hastily their previous good opinion 'from one who has served his country with fidelity and success'.

Pitt's statement reversed the people's misjudgement. On his resignation Pitt had been deluged with the tokens of city freedoms. One address praised him as the minister 'who had roused the ancient spirit of this nation, and by integrity and steadiness united us at home and carried the country's reputation to a height unknown before, by our trade accompanying our conquests to every quarter of the globe'.

In November 1762 Pitt attended the Lord Mayor's Banquet, at which the King and Bute were guests. Pitt's successor was nearly mauled by the mob, despite his bodyguard of hired ruffians. The people gave Pitt a vociferous welcome, and to another guest, Robert Clive, 'it seemed as if King William instead of King George had been invited'. Pitt wished he had not come.

Pitt's old colleague, the Duke of Newcastle, resigned from the government he had nominally led in May 1762, on the refusal of his colleagues to continue the subsidy to Frederick. Characteristically he had described the expedition to Havana as 'a wild goose chase'. His years in power had cost him four-fifths of his private fortune. But his system of preferment had brought worthy men to office; Pitt could not have waged and won the war without Newcastle's support.

The peace negotiations dragged on for months. Bute showed the self-confidence of the novice. The clumsy simpleton was no match for the experienced Choiseul, who persuaded Bute that the retention of all her conquests by Britain would make enduring peace impossible. It was beyond Bute's capacity to maintain them all. Choiseul had no use for colonies; he thought it better for a country to increase its strength by developing its own industries, a surprisingly modern view. King George was anxious to extricate Britain from her European commitments, and never again to underwrite the predatory activities of the King of Prussia. The King's policy represented a fundamental shift from the 'Old System' whereby Britain had sought to balance the European powers for her own advantage.

George III and Louis XV were both anxious to end the war. Neither wanted to abandon their allies. Prussia and Austria were locked in stalemate. In January 1762 Britain had advised Frederick to make peace on the best terms possible. He pretended he had been betrayed by the shameless perfidy of Britain's new ministers. Britain had fulfilled her engagements to the letter. Frederick well knew that the war could only be brought to an end by British and French agreement. He concluded peace with Austria, securing Silesia, the stolen territory he had fought to retain. Although Prussia had gained nothing from the war, she had established her reputation as a military power, an implication of fearful peril to Europe.

The preliminaries of peace were signed at Fontainebleau on 3 November and were ratified in Paris on 10 February 1763. Britain contented herself with moderate demands, retaining Canada, Senegal, St Vincent, Tobago, Dominica and the Grenadine Islands, and receiving Minorca back in exchange for Belle Ile. France recovered Martinique, Guadeloupe, St Lucia, Gorée and two islands in the Gulf of St Lawrence, Miquelon and St Pierre. In India she was allowed to retain the factories held prior to 1749. Spain recovered Manila and Havana, in exchange for Florida, and received Louisiana from France.

King George called it a 'noble peace'. Lord Granville, speaking from his death-bed, described it as 'the most glorious war and the most honourable peace this nation ever saw'. Pitt charged that the terms of peace 'obscured all the glories of the war, surrendered the dearest interests of the nation, and sacrificed the public faith by an abandonment of our allies'.

Enfeebled by four years of unremitting labour and tortured by gout, Pitt dragged himself to the House of Commons to speak in the debate on the peace terms. His legs and feet were wrapped in flannel, his hands encased in thick gloves, his face pale and emaciated, his voice scarcely audible. He rose, he said, to give the House his personal and individual opinion, which he felt honour-bound to do, 'after the part I have taken in affairs'. He objected to the concessions made whereby France recovered her West Indian islands and her Newfoundland fisheries, on the fundamental principle (of which the ministers seemed to have lost sight) 'that France is chiefly, if not solely, to be dreaded by us in the light of a maritime and commercial power'. By restoring France's possessions 'we have given her the means of recovering her prodigious losses and of becoming once more formidable to us at sea'. Pitt

castigated the government for deserting King Frederick, 'the most magnanimous ally this country ever had'. Pitt spoke for three hours and twenty-five minutes. The House became weary and restless. On division it voted by 384 votes to 65 to approve the peace terms. Bute fell from power two months later, 'crushed by his own peace terms', his contemporaries jibed.

Under Pitt's expert guidance, Britain had consolidated and won

Caricature, 1761, lampoons the secret negotiations which failed to lead to open peace talks.

The ever-memorable Peace-Makers settling their Accounts.

a great trading empire on which the sun would not set for two centuries. He had turned defeat into triumph, protected the American colonists and made Britain a great power. Now Britain would have to defend that empire against jealous rivals, and even her friends. As the Duke of Bedford had predicted, the Americans, freed from the nightmare threat of French invasion, sought and gained their independence. As Pitt had foreseen, France rose from defeat again to challenge Britain, the revolt of the Americans giving her the opportunity to do so. Choiseul had rebuilt her navy, whereas Britain had allowed her own to stagnate. Intervening in the domestic quarrel, France lost a naval battle but won her war. She bankrupted herself to humiliate Britain, and her ships carried back from across the Atlantic the new spirit of freedom, the spark that ignited her own revolution.

Pitt lived for another fifteen years, in the opinion of some historians his greatest years, when he undertook the noble task of trying to reconcile British and American differences and to prevent fratricidal war.

Select Bibliography

Bradley, A. G.: *The Fight with France for North America*, London, 1900

Carlyle, T.: *The Battles of Frederick the Great*, London 1892

Corbett, Sir J. S.: *England in the Seven Years War*, London 1907

Davies, A. M.: *Clive of Plassey*, London 1939

Frégault, G.: *Canada: the War of the Conquest*, London 1969

Gipson, L. H.: *The Great War for Empire*. 10 vols., London 1941–1972

Hotblack, K.: *Chatham's Colonial Policy*, London 1917

Kimball, G. S.: *William Pitt's Correspondence with Colonial Governors in America*. 2 vols., London 1906

Knowles, Sir R. L.: *Minden and the Seven Years War*, London 1914

McCardell, L.: *Ill-Starred General* (Braddock), London 1958

McLennan, J. S.: *Louisbourg from its Foundation to its Fall*, London 1918

Marcus, G.: *Quiberon Bay*, London 1960

Parkman, F.: *Montcalm and Wolfe*. 2 vols., London 1884

Robertson, Sir G. C.: *Chatham and the British Empire*, London 1946

Savory, Sir Reginald: *His Britannic Majesty's Army in Germany During the Seven Years War*, London 1966

Sherrard, O. A.: *Lord Chatham: William Pitt and the Seven Years War*, London 1955

Taylor, W. S. and Pringle, J. H.: *Correspondence of Lord Chatham*. 4 vols., London 1838–40

Williams, B.: *William Pitt, Earl of Chatham*. 2 vols., London 1915

Index